From Savannah to Hollywood and Back Again

From Savannah to Hollywood and Back Again

Helen Cranman

Savannah, GA
2015

Copyright 2015
Helen Cranman
Cover design by Erik Casillas
Drawings by Helen Cranman
Published with the assistance of Stephanie Jackel
   and Printer's Ink

All rights reserved. No part of this publication may be reproduced in any form or by any means without the prior written permission of Helen Cranman,
5450 Abercorn Street, Apt. 323, Savannah GA 31405.

ISBN-13: 978-0-692-58645-7
Library of Congress Control Number: 2015959043

Herman and Helen, June 1945

Dedication
and
Herman's Love Letter

I would like to dedicate this memoir to my husband, Herman, who has always been able to see my potential. He has loved me when I really didn't know what my great appeal was. I have been fortunate to be able to return that love. We are like two parts of a puzzle that fit together. Our love flows between us like cool streams winding their way through life, running deeply and passionately.

During World War II, in July, 1944, when I heard Herman's B24 was shot down over Hungary, I made a promise to G-d that I would trade my life for his, if he came back. I would do my very best to make him happy. He did bail out, then spent ten months as a prisoner of war. When he came back, we were married. He wrote a letter of his love to me that contained the most beautiful words I have ever heard.

Today we are even happier than we have ever been. So, this is from my Honey, who always had faith in me.

To My Wife Helen:

We were children when G-d opened my eyes to your beauty and then to your goodness, for as I remember, love flowed over me as a gentle springtime breeze, and it was then that I knew my life had begun. Over the years young love grew ever stronger as heaven took part, sending three children, one by one, making me proud as can be. They each blossomed as we knew they would and took part of my love with them. Then again like the feeling one has while listening to lovely music, my love for you deepened even more, as again we were blessed with children's children, each an unfinished beautiful melody they seemed to be.

In looking back I am overwhelmed by G-d's kindness in giving you to me and to the lifetime of love and happiness we enjoyed, and that continues to grow as we age. I cannot imagine what my life would have been without you, and I have no words that can fully express how wonderful my life with you has been these many years, but maybe it can be compared to the beauty found in a magnificent sunset, which is the one thing that comes close enough to express how I view our lifetime.

I will always love you.
Herman

Table of Contents

Beginning the Story
Setting the Stage	3
The Beginning of My Story	7
Goldie Davis Schmalheiser and Joseph Schmalheiser	16

Early Days in Savannah
My Awakening	25
The Birthday Party	30
The Emperor's New Clothes	34
Being Salesladies in Winner's Department Store	36
When I Met Albert Einstein	38
My Uncle Dave Finn	41
When the Girl Scouts Spent the Night Out	43
Grandma Davis and the City Market	47
Lord Have Mercy	51
Grandma and Grandpa Schmalheiser	54
Grandpa's Bathtub	59
Floradora and My Great Aunt	61
The Bi-lo Baby	72

Tybee Tales
Riding the Train to Tybee	79
The Iceman, the Vegetable Man, the Fish Lady, and the Milkman	82
The Tybrisa Pavilion	84
Topless in Tybee	86

Hollywood
    Packing Up – California, Here We Come   91
    California, Here We Are   107
    At the Office and Other Things   114
    Going to Glamorous Hollywood Places   127
    Heavy Hearts   130
    Going to the Academy Theater   133
    My Cousin Bobby Small   144
    My Uncle Eddie   148
    Going to Lunch With Aunt Elsie   154
    Arthur's Proposal and Our Wedding   159

Back in Savannah
    Who Are You?   171
    The Next Sixty-Six Years   174
    What I Did for the Community   183
    My First Trip to Washington, D.C.   185
    Nancy Hanks, the Train   187
    When Herman Gave Me Chocolate Candy   190

The Rest of the Story
    My Honey   195
    Our First Grandson, Matthew   198
    And the Children, Grandchildren,   200
        and Great-Grandchildren

Poems
    Poems   207

My Paintings   219

Foreword

Savannah has been my home since birth, except for a couple of years when my parents decided to move to Beverly Hills, California, in September 1943. My father was going to work for his brother who was in the movie industry.

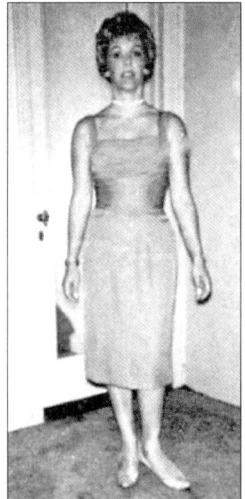

Helen Schmalheiser Cranman

While living there, I attended Woodbury College. I also worked for my uncle, Morris Small, at the Small Company, a theatrical agency and a subsidiary of Edward Small Productions, which belonged to another uncle, Edward Small.

Herman came home after the war in Europe ended, and we were married. When the war with Japan was over, we were able to return to Savannah where Herman joined his father in the family's insurance agency. Our three children, Paul, Lynn, and Roy, began arriving in 1947. We watched them grow up, becoming responsible, loving people, as we knew they would.

The purpose of my book is to pass on family history, and provide a portrayal of our lives, before and after we were married. I hope to provide stories that were told to me by my parents, grandparents, aunts, cousins, or friends. If mine vary from theirs, it is what I remember. So be it.

Beginning the Story

Setting the Stage

The whole thing started with a little ol' turnip sandwich. One afternoon as I read the paper to confirm what I'd heard during the day, I read the local column, "Around Town." There was a paragraph about a man who ate turnip sandwiches. (It neglected to say whether they were raw or cooked.) Anyway, ugh! Our columnist seemed to think "vegetable" sandwiches like that were very unusual. I could think of a dozen—cucumber and mayonnaise, watercress and relish, avocado and onion, nasturtiums and jelly, just to name a few.

Later on, the next day, I saw my columnist friend, Steve. I told him that I used to take avocado and onion sandwiches when I went to school in Beverly Hills. Also, how my friend brought the watercress (*hedge*, as Daddy called it) on rye with relish.

He listened to me. Once I got started, there was no stopping me. The key that unlocked the door to a whole flood of experiences had been found. I was off like a race horse. Ten thousand words were and are a minimum for me when I get started.

After a few of my stories, Steve managed to interrupt me to say he thought I should write about all these things that had happened to me. I still don't know if he was serious or just in a hurry. His parting words to me were, "Helen, take my word for it. It will dog you 'til you do." This was in 1959.

I shrugged my shoulders in amusement, but he was right. It did, but it took my three offspring to spur me into action.

Every morning as I stood at the stove, I don't know why, but when I broke the eggs into the frying pan, their yokes sunny side up hypnotized me. Before I realized it, I was off in a fog, flying across time and space. For a brief moment I'd visit California seeing

Mama, Daddy, my two sisters Elinor and Miriam, and their little ones. I tried to think what they would be doing that day or perhaps of things that happened in the past, so many wonderful times.

One morning, after a conversation with my newspaper friend, I was off on my magic carpet. As I turned the eggs, thoughts spilled out of my brain faster than I could think. Steve was right. I wanted to rush to my typewriter.

I stepped over children. I dropped things. I stepped back over the children. They sensed my preoccupation that day because they were full of many more questions than usual.

"Mother, where are my socks?"

"Mama, I can't find the belt to my dress."

"Mommy, I want my cereal."

This went on for a few moments. I ignored them, getting plates for the eggs, fixing toast, coffee milk, and so on. Finally, they retreated in silence. I could feel their eyes staring at my back. They started to whisper to each other.

Roy, who was four, said, "Is she sick?"

Lynn, the ten-year-old, assumed the mother role, feeling I was certainly shirking mine and acting as if she knew I wasn't capable. "No dear, she's just thinking again. She won't answer you when she's thinking."

Paul, thirteen and a first class Boy Scout, said, "What the heck is she always thinking about? She never answers, just walks around with that blank stare, not looking at anything. Boy!"

Lynn whispered back. "Well, I'm not sure, but I heard her talking to Daddy. I think she's going to write a book about her life."

Setting the Stage

"Her life! You're kidding." he doubled over with laughter.

"Whatever for? Who'd read it?"

"Well, us, I guess. We'll have to."

I did come out of my lethargy long enough to become furious. The nerve! As I turned to tell them a thing or two, I realized how incongruous it must be for them. I was standing there in my quilted housecoat, flannel pajamas, socks with slippers, curlers in my hair, groggy-eyed.

I thought, "What could have ever happened to me that was exciting, much less glamorous, or interesting? Hmph," I said to myself, "it's time to show these children. What do they know of the lights of Hollywood the beauty of Beverly Hills and the interesting life the people there lead? When I mention Robert Taylor or Charles Boyer, they'd ask, 'Who are they?'"

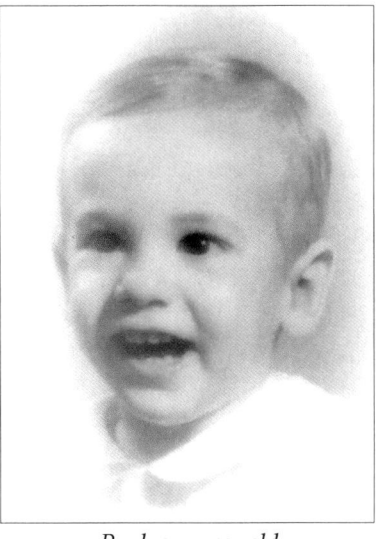
Paul, one year old

Oh, they've been to visit Nana and Grandpa in California, but the only movie stars they have ever met personally are Lassie the dog and Fury the horse. Boy...they think they're the last word!

I won't start at the beginning of my life because I don't remember anything about that, but Mama says when I was born, Grandma and Grandpa sent a telegram from California, where they were visiting Uncle Eddie, and asked that I be named Hermanine in

Lynn at one year

memory of my great grandfather whose name was Herman Lewin.

"Well," Daddy said, "Schmalheiser as a last name is plenty." Anyway, he'd just as soon have named me Strychnine or Turpentine.

Really, that's just what he said. Fortunately I ended up as *Helen*. Thank goodness for that, too, since my name would have been Hermanine Schmalheiser. I would never had a date, much less have gotten married.

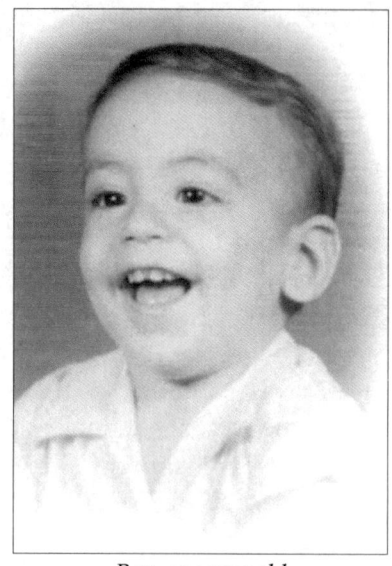

Roy, one year old

The Beginning of My Story

I was the second daughter born to Goldie and Joseph Schmalheiser, on May 17, 1925, in a hospital located on Drayton Street in Savannah, Georgia. I arrived feet first with the umbilical cord wrapped around my neck. I'm sure it was difficult for both Momma and me. I don't think she ever forgave me. A church later replaced the hospital. Daddy always joked about my being born in the last pew.

My sisters and I were very different. Miriam, the oldest, had curly red hair the color of spun gold and she had the most beautiful face. I was born when she was three. My sister Elinor arrived seven years later, with black curly hair, and was also beautiful. There I was sandwiched in between these two with my straight brown hair. I was cute, though, with lots of personality. I had a mouth that wouldn't quit. I was tiny for my age, had an opinion on everything and never failed to offer it.

Miriam, 5, and Helen, 2

Miriam was always the meticulous one, with starched dresses, white or black patent leather Mary Jane shoes and that gorgeous red hair all in curls. As for me, I hated all those things. I preferred climbing trees and fences, or jumping off the storage shed in the back yard. Momma finally put overalls on me. They weren't fashionable like they are today; only farmers and their sons wore them then. I didn't care until I learned boys liked girls in pretty dresses, with curly hair. So I changed my ways thereafter, and discovered the pleasure of being a girl.

I did like to dance and sing. When I was about three or four, I would go into the living room, wind up our Victrola record player (there were no electric ones then) and dance or sing to the song, "Ramona."

I will give my mother credit for starting me with dancing at a very early age: tap and ballet. I was pretty good at tap, but not at ballet. She sent me to ballroom dancing, too. I loved them all. She took me to elocution classes where I learned to speak and act like a lady. All my life, it gave me the confidence I needed when talking to a groups or taking part in local theater activities or college plays, in which I participated.

Miriam 7, Helen 4

Our family moved into a house my daddy built in a new development called Ardsley Park, the year before I was born. At that time, it was Savannah's southern-most outskirts. Since Miriam suffered with asthma, the doctor decided living there was bad for her health, so we moved downtown to an apartment on West Gwinnett, right next to the corner of Barnard Street. That was where my memories of life began. I was about four. Most of our friends lived nearby, so I was a happy little girl. My mother's parents lived two blocks away. My father's parents lived four blocks in another direction, making life very enjoyable.

My best friends, Phyllis and Audrey, lived across the street. Then our friend Cherie moved from New York to Savannah to live by

The Beginning of My Story

us, also. We have been friends ever since. At this time it's been over eighty years. At that time most Jewish families lived from West Liberty Street to West 37th, and from Bull Street to Barnard Street, to be close to their synagogue. This was from the time Jews first came to Savannah. When you walked east from West Gwinnett Street, you came to Forsyth Park, which was the largest, most important park in town, as it still is. East Gwinnett Street continued on the other side of the park. Many big beautiful houses were built there, some facing the park.

Helen with her father

Savannah has always been very cosmopolitan for a small Southern town. If there were any prejudices, most people kept their opinions to themselves. I don't ever remember my Christian friends saying unkind things to me because I was Jewish. My parents never said anything against other people either.

I went happily along doing all kinds of things, such as hanging off the flag pole from the second story window at the Meddins' apartment. We liked to stuff a stocking, sometimes the babies' Dr. Denton pajamas, with newspaper or fill balloons with water. Phyllis, Audrey, and I would tie a string to them, hanging them over the upstairs porch railing to scare people coming by.

We three girls played football with the boys across the street. I never caught the ball. We did play card games, rode our tricycles, or made rubber-band guns. Well, the boys made them for us, and we "shot" each other.

Some of my fondest memories of that period were about our neighbor, Mrs. Von Ebenstein, who lived across the street. We sat on the ground in her yard where she taught us about cleaning her pots with steel wool, water and backyard dirt until they shined. Then she would give us German cookies and lemonade.

Afterward, we went home covered with mud. Lottie, our housekeeper, fussed at us for getting messy. By that time she had already cleaned the bathroom, which meant that she had to scrub the tub all over again after bathing us. She would usually mumble something like, "I can't believe I'm working my fingers to the bone while you childrens are over there cleaning pots, getting dirty, making me have to scrub those knees to get you clean."

I went to kindergarten at the Jewish Educational Alliance (JEA) on Barnard Street. Our kindergarten class was held in the basement of the building. There were windows up high all around the room, where light and air came in. A prism hung up high in one of the windows so when the sun hit it, different colors flashed.

Miriam and Helen

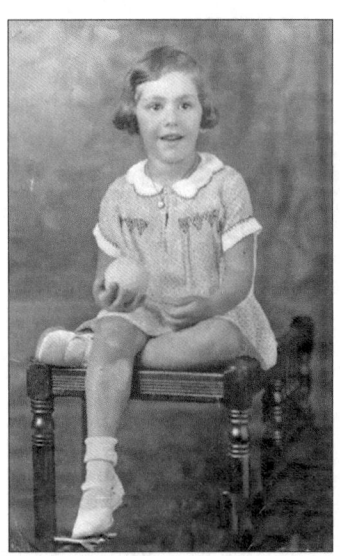

Helen at about 6

We went out in the square in the front of the building at break time to play games, such as: Ring-Around-the-Rosie; Drop the Handkerchief; Red Rover, Red Rover, Come Right Over; hopscotch, and jump rope. Sometimes we just chased each other. We learned our ABCs, sang songs, and listened to Bible stories. We celebrated all the Jewish holidays.

My friends were there, so that made it fun for me. Phyllis and Bubba, a boy we knew, were always in trouble, having to sit in the corner. Audrey and I stuck together because we were a little younger.

The Beginning of My Story

I began first grade at Barnard Street School, which was dark and dreary. The windows were large but my memories are of unpainted halls and walls. Maybe I should have been paying more attention to my studies.

Next we moved to East Anderson Street, where I went to Waters Avenue School. It was pure heaven in comparison to Barnard. I could walk to school, which was a block away. The building was beautiful. It had large windows, white walls, and the sun shined in all day.

This was where I first met Herman. I was five or six, and he was maybe a year older. I remember sitting on his doorstep across the street, waiting for him to come out to play with me, but he seldom did. He never remembered it was me until I told him decades later. The only thing he remembered was one time he helped boost some little girl over a fence, never forgetting how soft her "tushy" felt; that was me.

I stayed there all through grammar school. Even though we moved to a house on East 40th Street, I still went to the same school, walking to and fro. That was about ten blocks. Nobody ever drove me there in a car, even in bad weather. I had a raincoat.

Heller's Drugstore was operated by Herman's aunt and uncle, on East 40th Street. They lived with their two sons, Haskell and Rupert, in a house next to the store. Herman and his younger brother, Alvin, were frequent visitors. Whenever they were playing outside, I generally tried to take part in whatever they were doing, but it was a wasted effort, because they wanted nothing to do with girls. Decades later I asked Herman about it and all he would say was that he remembered some little girl who was always hanging around who had a big mouth. If it was me, I haven't changed.

Living there, we played kick the stick under the street lights after dark with some of our friends. Rupert and Haskell did things like riding their bicycles off the pitched roof of our garage, or catching flies to put in soda straws, and then they set both ends on fire.

That's where we taught my little sister, Elinor, to walk at ten months. It was also there that I had an emergency appendectomy at

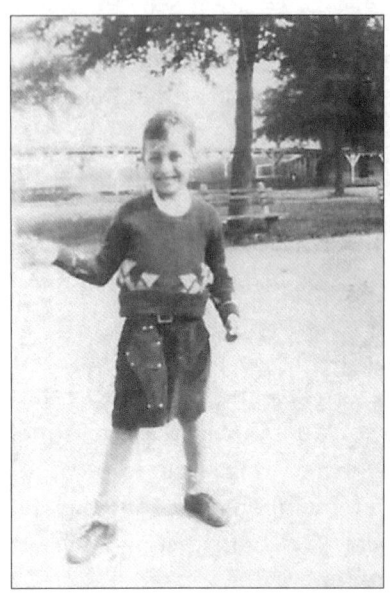 

Herman, 6 *Helen, 5*

eight years old. I woke up one morning and I couldn't move, being in terrible pain. I was taken to Dr. Henry Levington's office. He said I needed to go to the hospital. He would be there as soon as he got a haircut. A haircut? *A haircut?* I hoped he would make it. He told us later that as he took my appendix out, it burst open in his hand. That was before there were any antibiotics.

I was thirteen when we moved back to the house on 45th Street. I went to Richard Arnold Junior High School on Bull and 35th. By then Herman was following me down the hall, forgetting my soft tushy, but concentrating on other parts of my anatomy, since I was quite developed by twelve.

Later I went to Savannah High, which was a beautiful new school. It was two blocks from our house on 45th Street. I graduated in June 1943. I started going to Armstrong College, but since we moved to California that fall, I gave it up shortly after the classes began.

Life was enjoyable in Savannah. We had parties, went on dates and played poker for pennies when we lived at the beach in the summer. We grew up having fun through our teenage years.

The Beginning of My Story

One has to realize how incredible it is, being descendants of people who came to this country earlier in the 19th century. Living in the South had a lot to do with a better life. Everyone here had their little piece of land, whether a house in town, or a farm in the country. In Savannah we have the kind of weather where you can go out any time of the year to play games.

In all our years of marriage, I did volunteer work, but mainly took care of our three children, Paul, Lynn, and Roy. The next forty years were spent car-pooling for my own, then for my grandchildren, but I still managed to squeeze in a lot of fun things to do.

Our children and I participated in the Little Theater, Savannah's amateur playhouse. I did small parts, painted scenery, made costumes, danced or sang with the chorus.

I was also on the mayor's committee for making real movies. I found locations and recruited extras for the films. At times I also worked as an extra. Some of the films were *Cape Fear*, *The Color Purple*, *Bingo Long and the Traveling All Stars*, *Glory*, *Gator*, *Bernice Bobs Her Hair* (where I got screen credits), and others. I studied drama, writing, and art at the local colleges and also studied with some nationally-known artists.

After I found out that my best talent was painting, I stuck with that. I had one-man shows at W & J Sloane in Beverly Hills, the Los Angeles Home Show, the Pinehurst Country Club at Myrtle Beach, South Carolina, Savannah Art Association, the Senate building in Washington, D.C., the Association of Georgia Artists, Telfair Art Museum, and The Landings Art Association at Savannah, winning awards in many of the exhibitions in which I participated.

I also took dancing through the years for exercise. In my later years I tap-danced with a group called the Hot Flashes; we used to entertain the nursing home patients. I also had a business career with some success, but my first back surgery in 1969 ended that. I've done a little bit of everything including a small antique shop, selling real estate, and putting women in jobs as an employment counselor in Savannah. In 1969, working for a national firm, I put more women in jobs in Savannah than anyone in the United States.

From Savannah to Hollywood

After living in Los Angeles and seeing what someone goes through to get into professional acting even with tremendous talent, I realized I didn't have that much desire or ability. It's a passion to want something so desperately that nothing else in life matters. In the thirties and forties, you had to be in a big city with a stage mother to tackle show business.

Would you believe that this little girl from Savannah, Georgia, would go to Hollywood, live there for a couple of years having an exciting, wonderful time, only to realize that the one thing she wanted to do was to marry her honey and forget about Show Biz, and then go

Tap-dancing with the Hot Flashes

The Hot Flashes

back home to Savannah? It constantly amazes me how my life turned out. I couldn't wait to leave Savannah to travel and see the world, but I was glad to come home again.

Getting married, being able to have children, then grandchildren and great-grandchildren, turned out to be the best decision for me. My Herman was in charge of the Savannah Council on World Affairs and is also a hell of a writer. He just decided to sit down, write about being a prisoner of war, including our romance. He published it as *A Measure of Life.* The Mighty Eighth Air Force Museum has sold over two thousand copies of his books.

The Beginning of My Story

We pay for printing the books. The money from the sales goes to a fund we have in memory of our grandson, Matthew, sending history teachers to Europe and Israel, to study about the Holocaust.

Savannah, like any city, is a potpourri of different kinds of people. The city is divided east and west by Bull Street, which runs south from the Savannah River to the Forest River in White Bluff, a small community.

General Oglethorpe designed Savannah in 1733 with twenty-four squares, so that small forts could be built for shelter against Indian attacks. The Indians were friendly though, so the squares became parks.

Goldie Davis Schmalheiser and Joseph Schmalheiser

Goldie Davis Schmalheiser, my mother, was born in New York City, on January 15, 1903. She died in Savannah in January 2004. Her family moved to Savannah when she was very young. She had a sister Charlotte and a brother Milton. Her father, my grandpa, had five sisters, and he had to wait until they were all married before he could marry Grandma. I guess that was a Jewish custom in those days. It took ten years.

Charlotte, Goldie, and Milton Davis

Momma went to Anderson Street grammar school and to high school on Bull Street where the Board of Education is today. Next she went to Draughn's Business School which is now South College. She worked as a secretary at Neal-Blun, which sold building supplies, until she married Joseph Schmalheiser. She helped my father, took care of us, and did lots of volunteering. She could do anything she set her mind to. My momma said, "Nobody knows whose tomorrow it is." We figure she was the only one who knew the answer to that, because she lived longer than anyone else (101).

Uncle Morris, Uncle Eddie, and Daddy (Joseph) all danced and sang in the vaudeville shows at the Savannah Theater. They had been seen there by my mother's family. My Grandma Davis said they saw the cutest little man (my daddy). Also when Goldie

GOLDIE AND JOSEPH SCHMALHEISER

and her parents were returning to Savannah from New York by boat, they met Mrs. Philip Schmalheiser from Savannah, who said she would like Goldie to meet her son, Joseph. She did.

My parents were both active in the Savannah community. My mother worked for different charitable organizations, helping many of the German refugees find places to live when they came here before World War II. She did things for the soldiers stationed in Savannah. I went with her as two more hands, which always seemed to be my job in the family.

My father was born June 16, 1895, in Savannah. He was the fourth child in a family of seven. The children were Morris, Eddie, Hattie, Joseph, Lillian, Margie, and Freda (who died as a teen-ager). My father didn't get very far in school, going to work for my grandfather at a very young age. However, when he was a teenager (1912), he went to New York to work for Uncle Eddie.

Lillian, Hattie, Margie, Fredia, and Joseph Schmalheiser

Daddy stayed in New York for a while, but was sent back home to Savannah to help take care of my grandparents and his sisters. He went into his father's roofing business. He went into the Army in World War I, serving in France. After the war he came back to Savannah, met my mother, Goldie, and they were married.

My parents' generation didn't tell much about their growing up. One story Daddy tells is that when he was very young, he and his brothers went to the doctor and all had their tonsils out, then walked on to school. Did it cost less to have it done as a group?

Another story is that he was horseback riding as a young man. The horse threw him and came back home, taking someone back to where Daddy was lying on the ground, unconscious. He was brought home, where he remained unconscious for three days. Grandpa wouldn't call the doctor, saying, "He'll be all right." He was.

My father wanted to serve in the First World War. Unfortunately he weighed too little, so he could not get into the Army. When he was turned down, he went home, ate a bunch of bananas, and weighed more, so they accepted him. He was the first person in our family to go to college. The Army sent him to the University of Georgia in Athens for training.

I asked Daddy to write how he and Momma met. He wrote:

Goldie and Joseph Schmailheiser

> We met in 1920 after WWI at a dance in Savannah. She couldn't give me a date the first week. She was a Girl Scout, so she had to usher at different affairs that came up at the city auditorium. I had a bad habit of playing cards on the weekends. I tried to get dates with her. Finally I had to give up the cards. She gave up ushering. That worked. We went together for about a year, getting married on September 1, 1921. We have called each other "Sweetheart" for over sixty years.

My mother tells her story:

> In the year we saw each other in Savannah, we went to Tybee or Thunderbolt for our dates. There were places to eat and dance. Joe had a Buick car. I worked for Neal Blun Company as a secretary. After we got married, I helped Joe in his business and raised our three daughters. We lived in Savannah until 1943, when the war put us out of business. We couldn't get materials. The men left us to work for the shipyards. Joe's mother had died by then. His father moved to Florida with Margie, Joe's sister. Joe got hurt at the shipyard where he worked, so he went to California to visit his brothers and sisters to recuperate. He loved it so much, he called me saying, "Sell everything, and come to California." I put up our home for sale, our place of business, and two

trucks. I sold the house in no time, for cash. I called the train station asking about moving to California. The man I talked to told me I could rent a freight car to move our furniture, and put our car in it, also. When our freight car left for California, Helen, Elinor and I went to North Carolina to visit my sister, Charlotte, and her family. We took the train to Los Angeles, arriving on November 15, 1943. When the furniture arrived, we moved out of our furnished apartment into the house we bought on Willaman Drive in Beverly Hills with Helen and Elinor. Our daughter Miriam had married before we left Savannah and was with her husband Hymie in Alabama (he was in the Army). Joe went to work for his brother until he retired in 1971 and we moved to Laguna Hills, California, where we lived until his death in 1984.

Daddy always said, "Life is just one damn thing after another!" Truer words were never spoken.

We three girls got married. Miriam and Elinor stayed in Los Angeles, but Herman and I returned to Savannah to raise our family. We had our three children, eleven grands and now eleven great-grands.

Joseph died in September 1984. Goldie returned to Savannah in 1987. She lived in nursing homes in Savannah and Jacksonville, until her death in 2004.

My Father, Joseph Berger Schmalheiser

He never raised his voice, except in song.
The songs were always melodic, beautiful, or fun.
He was small in stature, a little over five feet tall.
To those who knew him, he stood six feet high.
He had green eyes that sparkled, a ready smile,
Followed by a laugh so infectious,
You'd want to reach out and catch it.
He never met a person he didn't like.
From the famous ones to those who were not.
Lots of people liked or loved him too.
He was the son of immigrants.
He wanted to serve his country in the First World War,
Where because of his size,

From Savannah to Hollywood

It was difficult for him to get into the Army.
 But he made it.
He went to France as a foot soldier.
He didn't ask for much.
He worked all his life for his family.
He loved a good time.
Dancing and singing on the stage,
He was good at both.
He was faithful to his wife.
He didn't drink or gamble.
He smoked until he heard it was unhealthy,
Then he quit.
He always did the right thing.
A man who was impeccably dressed,
Whether wearing a sport coat
Or a five-hundred-dollar suit.
He never said anything unkind to anyone.
I don't think anyone was ever unkind to him.
He never spanked his children.
He raised them with their mother
In a kind, happy way.
Retiring at seventy-five after many years
In the production of
The movie and television industry,
He was content traveling, going to a ball game,
Or just being with friends and family.
When cancer hit, he accepted it,
Continuing to do much the same,
With a smile, a laugh, or just
Being content.
When he reached a point
Of no longer being able
To take care of himself,
At eighty-nine, he
Decided it was time to go.
"Do nothing for me
Except let me die with dignity."
Turning to the nurses and saying with love,
"Look at my beautiful family."
Then he turned over, dying peaceably,

GOLDIE AND JOSEPH SCHMALHEISER

As he had lived, no fuss, no problem.
This man was not without faults,
They were so few and minor,
They are never remembered.
They buried him on a hillside
Of a military cemetery in California,
They played "Taps,"
Giving the flag to his family.
The snow-capped mountains he loved so much
Overlook the spot where he lies.
He would have been proud.
He was the captain of his ship,
The general of his army.
For that we gave him a twenty-one-gun salute.

This man was my father.

Helen Schmalheiser Cranman
Savannah, Georgia
March 19, 1992

Helen's father with Rochester,
from the Jack Benny Show

Joseph Schmalheiser
as a teenager

Early Days in Savannah

My Awakening

It was a hot summer day in the 1930s. I was five years old. Kindergarten was over until fall. That morning I jumped up from bed, put on a playsuit with some of my favorite colors: lavender, yellow, and turquoise. I went into the dining room to eat my breakfast. No cereal for me. I would eat only peanut butter on crackers with a glass of chocolate milk.

At that time we lived upstairs in the apartment on Gwinnett Street. All the windows were open, but not even a small breeze was blowing. There was no air-conditioning in those days. The electric fans hummed in every room, but they didn't help much.

When it was that warm, Momma made us stay inside, out of the hot sun, so we wouldn't get polio. That is what people thought in those days. It probably kept us from getting sun stroke or sunburned, but not polio.

On this particular day, Momma decided to take our dog, Wee Tong, to the veterinarian. I wanted to stay home because Mattie, who did our laundry every Monday, was coming. I always looked forward to her visit. She washed the clothes in the back yard. The weather made no difference to her. In the summer heat or the cold of winter, she came.

With nothing to do that morning until Mattie came, I went into the living room. It was the coolest room in the house, because it was in the middle of the apartment. The room was very dark. The east wall had two windows that looked out on the siding of the house next door. The other three walls had doors in them. The opposite wall from the windows had a sofa, with an arm chair next to it. Both were covered in a matching fabric of gold and black striped velour. That's velvet with class. I loved the feel of it, so soft and smooth. A small Oriental rug hung on the wall over the sofa. It had an allover pattern in shades of maroon and blue and felt like feathers. The north wall had a bookcase by the door with a picture of Momma in a cloche hat. No matter where you went in the room, her eyes followed you. She wasn't smiling, either. The fourth, south wall had a door that led to the dining room. The only light to the living room came through that door. The apartment was very old, musty, with decay and staleness evident. There was a smell of darkness in the room. The fan was making a quiet whirring sound.

Momma in her cloche hat

I was sitting there on the sofa, in the dark, thinking about standing on my head so I could rub my bare feet on the Oriental rug. I did it all the time. I knew there would be trouble if Momma came home and caught me doing it. She wouldn't even let me put my hands on it, because she said they were dirtier than my bare feet. The temptation was overwhelming.

I would be able to hear Momma come in the front door as the dog's nails clicked on the steps. I was just about to stand on my head, when I heard Lottie, our housekeeper, humming in the kitchen as she cooked for the day. I thought she was too busy to bother about me, but suddenly she called out:

"Helen, honey, I see Mattie downstairs in the yard getting ready to make a fire so she can heat the water to wash the clothes." Lottie was looking out the kitchen window. "You need to take them down to her." I jumped off the sofa, running to get all the things out of the hamper.

Mattie, the laundry lady, was old. She needed me to "hep" her. That is what she made me believe, and it made me feel very important. I loved Mattie. Next to Lottie, she was my very best friend.

My Awakening

While I waited for Lottie to tie the clothes in a sheet, I went into the dining room to check on Daddy's canaries which he kept there in big cages. I fed and watered them. There were small round strainers filled with cotton attached to the sides. The females had laid eggs in them and we were waiting for them to hatch. The baby birds were ugly until they got feathers, looking like little worms.

When the clothes were ready, I dragged the bundle of laundry to the back door, off the dining room, leading to an outside wooden staircase, which was long, unsteady, unpainted, and uneven. I pushed the big bundle out the door, watching it bump down the stairway until it got to the bottom. Mattie caught it as it tumbled to the ground.

"You stay out of the sun. I don't want you to get polio, ya hear?" Lottie called, as I ran out the door, down the steps.

The house was built high off the ground, so I went under the back porch of the downstairs apartment to get the big #2 wash tub, and rolled it on its side to Mattie. Making several more trips with my red wagon, I got wood for the fire, while Mattie made a square out of some bricks on the shade side of the yard. In the middle of the wood she had kindling with newspaper all wadded up on top. We put the big washtub on the bricks. We brought buckets of water from the outside spigot to fill up the tub. Mattie lit the fire. When the water got hot, she put the clothes in, scrubbing them on the washboard with bar of Octagon soap. There were no detergents or washing machines in those days.

I wandered around the yard, barefooted, pulling up some pee-in-the-beds, a blooming weed. I put a flower under Mattie's chin to see if she had peed in the bed. If they reflected yellow under your chin, it was a sure sign that you had peed in the bed. Well, Mattie's chin reflected yellow. "Ooooo! Mattie!" I said. She laughed so hard she almost fell off her stool.

She walked over to the side of the yard, cutting two sticks, switch size. Out of the pocket of her apron, she took some marshmallows she had wrapped in a handkerchief. We put them on the sticks to roast in the fire. She sat down on her stool to rest for a few moments, wiping the sweat off her forehead with her apron. I climbed on her lap as we put our marshmallows in the fire to roast and eat. Afterward, I hugged Mattie. She scrubbed the rest of the clothes until they were clean. We poured out the water, got fresh water to rinse the clothes. Then we used the rinse water to douse the fire.

Mattie hung some clothes on the line, laying the rest around the yard on weeds for the sun to bleach while they were drying. Where the wash water made a mud puddle, I wrote my name, Helen, with my big toe.

After a while I got bored and decided to go back upstairs. I went halfway up the steps, climbed over the railing onto the roof that covered the porch of the downstairs apartment. I went into the house through the dining room window that overlooked the yard. I had been told not to do this many times. Lottie stood there with an unpleasant expression as I came through the window.

"You could have fallen off that roof, an' really hurt yourself. How many times have you been told not to do that?"

"I'm careful."

"Careful don't help none, if you wuz to fall."

I walked past her back into the living room, climbing on the sofa. Lottie followed.

"If you plan to put those dirty feet up on your mother's good rug, you better think about it again. I don't want to be here if Miz Goldie comes home an' catches you." Lottie knew me too well.

"I'll hear them coming up the steps." I said.

Lottie wore her hair pulled back in a bun and was very beautiful. She left the room shaking her head mumbling, "That chile's gonna be the death o' me." She didn't really mean it, because I knew she loved me. I loved her. She was light-skinned. She was Scotch, Irish, Native American, and African. She said that made her colored. Lottie went to school, but I don't think Mattie did, which made me sad. They were both real ladies, though.

After Lottie left the room, I stood on my head on the sofa. To balance, I put my dirty feet on the beautiful wall rug. It felt good, so soft. I can still remember. My playsuit was backless; I could feel the cool velour sofa on my back. When the blood rushed to my head, everything seemed different upside down. I looked around the room while rubbing my feet on the rug. I smelled the food cooking in the kitchen, and was aware of Lottie banging pots. Mattie came into the house to put up the ironing board in the dining room. I heard the floors creaking as they walked around. The noon sun came through the door from the dining room, giving everything an eerie color. It was a dreamlike moment, quiet and cool, still dark in there. I shut my eyes, breathing quietly and floating on a velvet sea. I was totally engrossed in my own thoughts.

Suddenly, I heard a noise. I opened my eyes. A huge figure loomed in the dining room doorway. The light was shining behind it. I couldn't tell who it was. It was as if G-d had walked into the room. I was stunned. I got goose bumps. I felt cold.

But, it wasn't G-d. Momma had come up the back steps and I never even heard her! She stormed into the living room as I slithered down off the wall to the sofa. Snapping her fingers on my behind, she said, "I thought I told you not to do that. Now you just sit there until I tell you to get up."

After she left the room, I didn't cry. I just sat there day dreaming. I looked at my hands, my feet and the clothes I wore. I felt the material on the sofa again. At that moment it was as if I had just come alive. It was the first time I was aware of being a person.

"I'M ME, HELEN."

I was really stunned at the realization. I am still unable to describe exactly how I felt. Perhaps it was blood rushing to my head, or Momma smacking my rear end. Who knows? It wasn't my birthday, but it is the day I feel I was born. Certainly it was when I became aware of life, the universe, and me. I didn't give a hoot about what Momma said. She fussed at me a lot, but I never listened to her. I was always my own person. It drove her nuts.

The Birthday Party

It was the day after Christmas. I was still the baby, spoiled by my family, my grandparents, and friends. When Hanukah and Christmas came to our house, the living room floor would be covered with toys. That same year I was given a red tricycle, and I thought it was the greatest. Savannah is cold in December, so Momma bundled me up in my coat, hat, and gloves. Daddy carried my vehicle down from our second floor apartment. I began riding on the brick sidewalk, which was all bumpy with holes, but I didn't care. I was having fun seeing how fast I could go from one end of the block to the other.

My best friend came over to see my trike. Trudging along behind was her big sister. She reminded me of my own big sister, bossy and acting all grown up.

"See what Santa brought me because I have been good all year."

I stuck my chest out with pride. My friend walked all around, touching the chrome handlebars and the red paint job. Her sister just looked at it with a "big deal" look.

"Shiny, isn't it? I love the red color, too." I was riding with no hands, my arms folded over my chest while I talked as my friend *ooooo*'d and *ahhhh*'d.

"Can I ride it some?" she asked, as she kept circling around me.

"All right" I answered, being very magnanimous. I rang the bell attached to the handle for her to get out of the way.

"Udden, udden," I said, thinking I sounded like a car motor.

Her sister stepped in my path, saying,

"Santa didn't bring you that bike. There isn't any Santa Claus. Even if there was he wouldn't bring you anything because you're Jewish. Your mother and daddy bought you that, so there. If there

The Birthday Party

was a Santa, he wouldn't come to our house, either, because we're Jewish, too."

My ears could not believe what I was hearing. She was making that up. I sat there stunned, staring at her, mouth quivering, tears forming. I could feel my heart breaking into a million pieces. I jumped off of my new tricycle, knocking it over in the process, running up the stairs as fast as my little feet could take me.

"Momma, Dee says there isn't any Santa. She said even if there was one, he wouldn't bring me anything because I'm Jewish. He's been coming to our house for a long time. I know she's wrong. She is, isn't she?" I cried.

Momma heaved a big sigh. She sat down on the bench at the head of the stairs, pulling me down beside her. "Well," she said, "it's like this: Santa is just a spirit, like a fairy. You never see him, but you can believe in him, even if you're Jewish. He comes from non-Jewish belief but he isn't a religious character or a real person. Daddy and I thought you were so good all year, that you deserved something nice."

So Dee was right. Well, that wasn't going to keep me from enjoying myself. I ran downstairs to play. My friend was riding my bike. She got off to let me have it. We took turns, one pedaling, and the other standing on the step between the back wheels. Her sister went away. My friend and I had fun.

What does that have to do with a birthday party? Well, during that same period, when any of the older girls had a birthday party, they had to invite all the little sisters and brothers. I don't know why, because the little ones didn't have to ask the big ones to their parties. I guess they didn't want to come.

Shortly after Christmas it was Dee's birthday. At the party she invited all her friends, which included my older sister, all the little sisters, plus one brother called Bubba. She was very unhappy about inviting the kids, but not as unhappy as I was. Dee didn't want us. I certainly didn't want to go, being the only child in history who hated ice cream and cake.

I complained to Momma, "Curl my hair. Wear a party dress. Take her a present. You know I hate birthday cake. I don't really care about ice cream unless it's the kind Daddy makes in the churn." It was true. I ate almost nothing. "Anyway, Mrs. Von Ebenstein is going to let us go in her backyard to clean her pots with sand. It's fun. Then afterwards she'll give us lemonade with German cookies."

Mother gave me that look. "If you want to clean pots, you can stay home, help with our pots."

At the birthday party; Helen is fourth from left.

"We don't have German cookies at our house." I sighed. I knew I had to go. I took my bath, put on one of my dresses and my black Mary Janes. I let Momma attempt to curl my hair. I walked across the street, all by myself, which I was allowed to do. My sister Miriam was already there. After the candles were blown out, we sang "Happy Birthday." We were served ice cream and cake; I didn't eat mine.

Dee started opening her presents. The big girls gathered around, tying the ribbons together to make a bouquet. The bunch of us little ones, all girls except Bubba, were finishing their ice cream and cake; we couldn't see what was going on, on the other side of the table, because we were sitting down. Bubba got bored. Suddenly he stood on his chair. Just we little ones noticed. Then he climbed up on the dining room table. We started to snicker and giggle.

Bubba started to shout:
Ladies and gentlemen take my advice!
Pull down your pants and slide on the ice.
Ladies and gentlemen
Matter of fact!
Pull down your pants and sit on a tack.

The Birthday Party

The silence was deafening. Dee was upset, to say the least. She said, "Bubba, you get down from there this minute. Momma, I told you I didn't want them at my party. Now, they've ruined it." She looked like she was about to cry,

"All you little kids get out of here," she added.

We were shooed into her mother's bedroom. We went, still giggling. Bubba thought he was great stuff. I loved ruining Dee's party, but banishing us to the bedroom with the door shut was a big mistake.

Bubba was nosey. One of Dee's mother's dresser drawers was open just a little bit. He opened it further. Then he said,

"Look what I found—chocolate."

Well, I'd eat that. I got up off the bed where I'd been sitting. He was so generous. He broke it up so we'd each have a nice size piece! After a while, the door was opened. We came out, each going to our own homes. I walked back across the street.

A few hours later I got deathly ill. I thought I was going to die from the pains and cramps in my stomach, along with diarrhea.

"What did you eat at the party? Did you eat the ice cream and cake?" Momma asked.

"Nooooo. Sister ate the ice cream and cake, but I didn't."

I doubled up, ran to the bathroom. When I came out, I said,

"Oh, I remember, I had a piece of chocolate candy."

My sister said, "We didn't have any chocolate candy."

"Well, I did. Bubba found some in the dresser drawer when we got sent into the bedroom."

"Why were you sent to the bedroom? Never mind. I don't think I want to hear that right now. You can tell me later. What kind of chocolate was it?" my mother wanted to know.

"I don't know, Momma, I didn't see the wrapping."

"Well, I'm calling Dee's mother right away," which she did.

As everyone can surmise, the chocolate was the laxative, Ex-Lax. In fact, all four of us got sick.

I guess you could say we got our comeuppance.

The Emperor's New Clothes

When I decided to write about my life for my family, I didn't know I would get stuck in the 1930s. Perhaps that decade sticks out in my mind because of many memorable events. Or perhaps because when a person gets along in years, your long-term memory works better than the short-term one.

David and Esther Finn with Helen

This story is about the time I went to college when I was five. At that time my Aunt Esther was in a play at our local college. The name of the play was, *The Emperor's New Clothes*. It's the well-known fairy tale about a stupid king who was convinced his tailor had made him the most elegant suit of invisible clothes. This dumb king decided to wear it, not realizing he was stark naked!

As he rode his horse in a parade, all the people in the streets were appalled, but this one little kid stepped out of the crowd saying, "But, he doesn't have on any clothes."

That little kid was played by me. I told everyone I was going to college to learn how to act. And I really believed it. I know that was probably when I decided I wanted to be a star. I was brilliant. Everyone told me so.

The Emporer's New Clothes

What makes this story really interesting to me is that the director was Stacy Keach Sr. He later went to Hollywood, where he became a director. I used to talk to Mr. Keach on the phone when I worked for my uncles in Hollywood. He remembered me. His son, Stacy Keach Jr. (who was born in Savannah), became a very famous actor. Seeing him in a movie on television recently reminded me of that part of my life.

Later there was a drama coach at the Jewish Community Center who cast me at age fifteen as Hannah in the story of *Hannah and Her Seven Sons*. In biblical times, Hannah and her children were told by the Roman king in Israel to bow down, kiss his ring, and become Christians. When they didn't, he just boiled them in oil.

This director, who was from Moscow, said I had talent. He wanted to give me drama lessons. My mother told me there were millions of people out in the world who tried to get into show business, but very few succeeded. I couldn't understand her attitude. She had always encouraged me before. As I write this story I think the real reason was that she didn't want me at the gentleman's apartment. She was probably right. I was so young in those days, I never thought of such things.

From that time, I have danced, acted, and tried to sing, but I have always been most successful with my art work.

Being Salesladies in Winner's Department Store

Throughout my younger years we visited Aunt Charlotte and Uncle Joe Winner in Morganton, North Carolina. Aunt Charlotte was really more like a big sister than an aunt to my two sisters and me. Our parents, the three of us girls, and Wee Tong, the family Chow dog, would pile into the car, driving to their house in the mountains. Sometimes in the summer, Momma and Daddy would leave the three of us girls there and return in a couple of weeks to take us home.

We went at Christmas time, too. My aunt and uncle owned a small department store. Miriam and I worked for them part of the time, usually on Friday and Saturday. She, being the older, would handle the cash register. I waited on customers, like the gypsies who came through Morganton at different times of year. They were so fascinating with their black hair, black eyes, and colorful clothing in reds and greens, with gold dangling from everywhere, ears, neck, arms. They were a sight, riding in their big Cadillacs, pulling trailers, causing a great commotion in that little city.

Elinor, who was too young to work, stayed home with our cousin Gene and the housekeeper.

Uncle Joe gave each of us a small cardboard suitcase. Then he let us fill it up with clothes. He also paid us, even though he knew we would have worked for nothing. What lucky little girls we were. We filled them up with clothes for school or shorts and whatever we needed for the beach in the summer, for which my parents paid.

I loved to visit the drugstore, a couple of doors down from Uncle Joe's store, to get an ice cream cone. I liked sitting there, talking to the young man who worked the soda fountain. I felt so grown up when I did.

One day a farmer parked in front of the store. He had a cow and a dog in the back of his pickup truck. I ran outside to pet the cow. Luckily, the dog didn't seem to mind. The farmer, who was dressed in overalls and a straw-hat, got out of the cab, spitting tobacco juice in the gutter as he went by. He came into the store with some cloth. He told me his wife wanted to make a dress, but she didn't have enough material, so she needed some more. The fabric he brought in was blue with little flowers. There wasn't any of that particular design left. We looked at all of the pieces, but I finally showed him some cotton material that "sorta" matched. It was the same color blue, but plain with no design. I asked him how much he needed. He didn't know. I asked how much she weighed. He told me about three hundred pounds.

"So you think that piece will do, do ya?" he asked.

"Yes, I certainly do." Then I explained how she could use one piece for the blouse and the other for the skirt.

"Well, you're a pretty smart little girl."

I was so little, I could hardly reach up on top of the table to get the material down. He helped and I measured four yards, which we decided he needed to be safe. I carefully folded it; taking it to the cash register for Miriam to ring up the sale.

"Four yards will be eighty cents. Thank you very much." He paid me and left.

Miriam said, "You sold that man material to go with the one he brought in and it didn't match? I can't believe you did that."

"Well, he was happy," I answered, being so proud of myself.

When I Met Albert Einstein

In the same era, some of the smart or lucky Jewish people got out of Europe before the Holocaust atrocities began. One family who came to Morganton, North Carolina, was the Einsteins: a couple who were grandparents to two very young girls. The children belonged to their son, living in Italy. He was married to an Italian woman, not Jewish. At that time Hitler had not reached Italy, though it was evident that he would. The little girls were sent to this country as a precaution. The grandfather was a chemist, working in fabric dyes, for the large furniture factories located in Morganton.

At the time they mostly stayed to themselves, but were friends with the people in the Jewish community. Since there were no little Jewish girls in Morganton, at their request my aunt sent me to visit their grandchildren whenever I came to Morganton. I would spend the day at their house. I was older, but they were very bright and spoke English, so we were compatible.

A lot of land surrounded their family's house. They had the biggest yard I had ever seen. Their property may have been a farm at one time. I loved the feeling of freedom, space, and sky. I taught the girls to play many games, including cowboys and Indians, which the girls loved, but it didn't go over too well with their grandparents.

On one of my visits, they received a phone call which caused much excitement because their uncle was coming to visit that very day. The house was turned upside down. We were given chores to do. We dusted furniture, swept the back porch, and emptied waste baskets. Scurrying around all morning, we did the things we were asked to do. Next we set the table for lunch. At noon we were fed our lunch, had our faces washed, our hair combed, and were sent out on the back porch to wait for the girl's uncle.

We couldn't do anything because we had to keep clean, so hopscotch and jump rope were out. We got their dolls, quietly playing house, while awaiting the arrival of this very important man. I kept going to the side of the house looking for an automobile. Finally one of the girls said, "He's not coming in a car. He always comes in an airplane."

Albert Einstein's letter to Franklin Roosevelt arning of the atom's inherent power resulted in the Manhattan Project, which built the Alamogordo device, code-named Trinity.

I said to myself, "This is really going to be something! Wow!" I tried to act as casual as they were, but it was hard. After what seemed to be an eternity, we saw a little speck in the sky. It looked like a mosquito and buzzed like one, too. A tiny two-seater single engine plane circled the big back yard and came down, landing just opposite the back door.

"Girls, don't go out there. Wait until the propeller stops going around and Uncle gets out of the plane." The door opened and a small thin man got out. He had brownish-gray unkempt hair, a dark mustache, with not too regular features. His suit was all wrinkled. His shoes looked too large and besides he didn't have on any socks.

Was he why we worked so hard all morning? The girls went running out to greet him, shouting, "Uncle Albert, Uncle Albert!" Their grandparents greeted him with hugs and kisses.

I stood watching. He leaned over to kiss them both. Then he motioned for me to come over too. He asked my name. Greeting me warmly, he extended his hand and shook mine. We exchanged "how do you do's."

The girls talked excitedly to him, as all of us walked to the house. He listened patiently. Then the grownups went into the house to eat their lunch. We ran back to the plane. The pilot let us climb in and out of the plane. After a while the grownups came out of the house. Their uncle kissed them goodbye. Getting in and sitting down, he waved as the plane rolled out for its take off.

When I went back to Aunt Charlotte's house that day, I was all excited.

"Did you have a nice day?" she asked.

"Did I? Well, it was the most exciting day of my life. Mr. Einstein's relative came. He came in a tiny airplane that landed right in their back yard. While he ate lunch with the grownups, the pilot let us climb all over the plane."

"So did they say who he was?"

"I don't know, but the girls kept calling him Uncle Albert."

"Albert Einstein! Albert Einstein! You met Albert Einstein?"

"That's what they called him. What's so great about that?"

"He's just one of the most brilliant men in the whole world. That's where those girls get their brains."

"Well, he sure didn't look smart. They acted like he was really important, but he didn't act that way."

I didn't think about that day until a few years ago, when I heard some third graders talking about him. They knew who he was and I was impressed with that.

The last time I talked to Aunt Charlotte, I wanted to make sure my facts were straight. She remembered that day, saying I was right. She said one of the girls became a ballerina and the other, a college professor. They never went back to Italy to live. I never heard what happened to their parents.

My Uncle Dave Finn

David Finn and his wife, Aunt Esther, were not really my aunt and uncle, but our families were very close. His wife's brother married my mother's sister, so that made us "family." They were wonderful people; she was very beautiful and kind. He was so tall, about six feet, handsome, with a winning smile and a personality to match. He was a customs inspector, so he wore a black uniform with brass buttons. A white hat topped the outfit. He was the only person I had ever known at that time who wore a uniform.

Whenever Uncle Dave saw me, he'd swing me in the air, put me on his shoulders, and take me for a walk. Other times he'd do magic tricks. He was a man never at a loss for words, always full of fun for a little girl. They never had any children, so they doted on my older sister and me; we had no younger sister then.

One day when I was a teenager, my momma and I were downtown shopping, when I saw Uncle Dave walking about half a block ahead of us.

"Momma, Momma, its Uncle Dave. Let's hurry so we can catch up with him."

Mother stopped me, saying, "No, he's with another man. They're probably talking about business. You can't bother him now. You'll see him soon."

Helen with Uncle David

"Momma, please, please, he won't care. He'll be glad to see me." My heart was broken, but I listened to her. I never saw him again!

About a month later, Uncle Dave and Aunt Esther went to see a football game at the University of Georgia in Athens. Uncle Dave drove with gusto, as he did everything else. On the way home, he rounded a curve, crashing into an unlit truck parked on the road. He was killed instantly. Aunt Esther survived, but was never the same.

Helen, AZA Sweetheart

I told my mother, "You should have let me see him. Now I will never get to see him again. I wish I could have seen his face."

After that, even to this very day, whenever anyone leaves me, I must see their face. When walking to the door, my husband, my children, their spouses, and all our grandchildren always look me in the face. They know it sort of makes me feel that they will be safe. G-d will take care of them if I see their faces before they go away.

The local AZA chapter was named in memory of him to honor his involvement with the Jewish youth of Savannah. This picture of me was in the *Savannah Morning News* when I was elected the first "Sweetheart of the David Finn Chapter of AZA." Aleph Zadik Aleph is the youth group of the national B'nai Brith organization. As the Sweetheart, I represented our chapter in the state meeting in Atlanta.

When the Girl Scouts Spent the Night Out

One summer in the early forties I had been a counselor at the Girl Scout camp. The camp director asked me if I would help a Girl Scout troop leader for the coming winter in town. However, that leader got married and pregnant right away, making me the leader of the group.

The girls came from less fortunate homes. Some were living in foster houses or in homes for girls.

We met in a basement apartment once a month. It was in the downtown area, within walking distance of where the girls lived. I got them all uniforms from girls who had outgrown theirs. They never missed a meeting, and they always got there before I did. All of them would be talking about their boyfriends, throwing their cigarettes in the fireplace (which was the mode of heat for our meeting room), so I wouldn't catch them smoking. As if I wouldn't smell it.

I was ready to teach them, *On my honor, I will try: To serve God and my country, To help people at all times, And to live by the Girl Scout Law.* The girls put their hands over their hearts. Then we said the

Helen (center) with Girl Scout troop

pledge to the flag. They didn't care, but I made them learn it because these were honorable ideals by which to live.

I decided we would learn things like how to do our fingernails, wash our hair, put on makeup, set a table, learn the different denominations of money, and so on. We walked to the YWCA, where there was a pool, and I taught them how to swim. I got some folks to take all of us to the beach, too.

Helen's mother, Goldie, was a Girl Scout (left, center row)

Then I got this brilliant idea that we should spend a night at the Girl Scout camp. It was off-season for the camp, so there would be room for us. I could try to teach them things they were supposed to learn in order to get a badge, like how to build a fire. We could roast marshmallows, cook hot dogs, tell ghost stories, talk about whatever we wanted. A lot of them had never done this before. I asked my mother to take some of us in the car. Daddy came with his truck, the rest of the group climbed in and off we went. Other troops were staying at camp, so they had the kitchen open for meals, but mostly we were off by ourselves.

It was in the spring of the year, warm, beautiful, with lots of flowers and trees in bloom. We chose cots in the cabins. Of course, there was one girl nobody would stay with, so I told her she could sleep in my cabin. That worked.

The next day after we had lunch, I collected them. "We're going on a hike," I announced. We put on our shorts. "Everyone get a buddy. Fill your canteens. Get in line. We'll march like soldiers." Off we went together. I decided I would lead them west from the main building, because when I had stayed at camp the summer before, I had never been that way. We walked for a while, picking up leaves to put together with sticks to make head bands so we would look like American Indians. We found oyster shells to glue together, planning to make pretty things for our families, also getting badges for being creative. We sang songs.

Someone found a shoe. We decided we would take it, fill it with dirt, and put a small tree in it. We sang more songs, marched for about ten minutes, when they started to go off in different directions.

"Stay within yelling distance, because if you go too far we will never find you, then you'll be lost forever." That scared some of them, but not others. So we walked a little longer, until people started getting thirsty. We stopped to drink from our canteens. It was a beautiful day. Some of the group went on ahead of us.

Suddenly there was a lot of screaming and yelling. I ran toward the noise, hoping no one was hurt. One of the girls came running toward me with a bone in her hand. "Look, a cow's leg!"

I looked at it. It wasn't a cow's leg. Janie, who knew everything, said, "That's a person's leg." They all started screaming, then running in all directions. "Wait," I said, "Come over here by me. I'll show you the right path to take back to the cabins." That stopped them in their tracks. Turning around, they all came. The girls stopped their carrying on but clung to me like little babies. After all, they were thirteen or fourteen years old. As I look back now, I realize that they were so young. I pictured myself as being very mature, although I was only seventeen years old at that time.

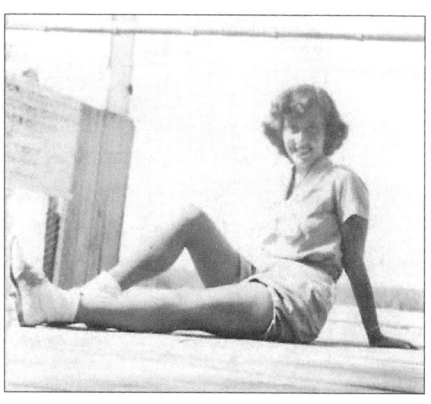

Helen on the dock at Scout camp

Janie said, "Fraidy cats, fraidy cats." I asked them, "Where did y'all get this?" They took me to a small brick crypt all alone in the middle of the woods. There were steps that went down inside. The door was ripped off, lying nearby in the leaves. Inside there was a small red metal casket with a glass top, evidently for a child. The glass was broken, and there was nothing in there. I didn't investigate too thoroughly.

"It was someone's grave. Some bad person broke in and stole things that belonged to whoever was buried in here," I offered as an explanation. The girls stood there saying, "How terrible." I felt so sorry for the little child. We put the leg bone back, picked up the door to the grave, leaning it over the opening. Some girls picked wild flowers to put there. We bowed our heads, each saying silent prayers.

"Well, let's go back and make a fire. We can write a story about this exciting adventure," I suggested. That's what we did. They couldn't wait to tell their families what they had seen. It was a very successful outing.

Today children go skiing on the slopes in Utah, or spend the whole summer at the beach, or go to Europe and Israel. There's so much to do, but that long ago experience was something to be talked about again and again by this group of underprivileged girls. That next fall I moved to Los Angeles with my family, never to see any of them again.

That summer as a counselor at camp, or working with that girls' group the winter before, were the first times I worked with a group of young people. Later on when I had my own children, I was a den mother for the Boy Scouts, which was a totally different experience.

Grandma Davis and the City Market

It was summer. My grandma Anna Davis was coming to take me with her to the City Market. Since she lived only a couple of blocks away from us, she walked to our house. We would catch the streetcar to town.

Momma was brushing my hair, wetting it, trying to make it curl. I was squirming as she did it, because I hated those stupid curls. "If you don't stand still and let me finish, you won't be ready when she comes." I stood still because I had already figured out that I would run in the bathroom before Grandma arrived to brush my hair straight.

The bell rang. It was her, but she didn't walk upstairs, because it was too many steps.

Grandma Anna Fisher Davis

"I gotta go to the bathroom," I yelled down to her, "then I'll be right there."

I went into the bathroom, grabbed my daddy's brush, climbed up on the toilet seat so I could see myself in the medicine cabinet mirror, and pulled the brush through my hair taking out the curls. Jumping down, I went to the linen closet, took out the white flavored mineral oil, which I liked, because it tasted like lemon custard ice cream. Taking off the bottle top, running my finger inside the bottle to get some to taste, I sucked the medicine off my fingers, and then I ran out of the bathroom, and down the steps, as Momma leaned over the banister yelling after me.

Grandpa William Gabriel Davis

"You want straight hair? You'll have straight hair. That's the last time I'll try to curl it to make you look pretty!"

"Good," I thought as I ran to meet Grandma, who had already walked to the corner.

We crossed the street to wait for the streetcar. My friend Larry lived right there in a big two-story house. He had a huge back yard that was not fenced in. In the middle of the acreage was his Shetland pony tethered to a big pole. He was black, brown, and white. I stood there petting him. He swished his tail as I hugged him around his neck. He bared his teeth. I knew he was smiling at me.

I saw the streetcar coming and I ran back, climbing aboard.

The windows were open. As I sat there, I remember the air blowing my hair. I felt cool, leaning back to enjoy the moment because I knew as soon as we got off I'd get all hot again. The sun was so bright it hurt my eyes. The car made its noise, "Clickity, clack, clickity, clack," as we tore down the street going at least twenty miles an hour.

When the streetcar got to the market it slowed down, putting on brakes, which made another sound, "Sheeeeeeeeesh," going inside the market, which it did in those days. In one side through the market and out the other, where it continued; turning around, going around the market, to go back to where it came from. We stepped down from the car, and our eyes didn't adjust to the darkness too quickly. For a minute we were overcome by a multitude of smells. It was a combination of fruits, vegetables, and flowers, with other odors from the chickens, pigs, cattle and horses.

I headed for the black ladies who were shelling peas, where I knew they would give me raw butterbeans or green beans to eat. Their men were peeling sugar cane; they gave me pieces to chew on. Farmers were selling corn, watermelon, and "wegetubbles" as some of the black people who spoke Gullah called them. I understood Gullah. It was almost our native language. Gullah is a combination of 17th century peasant English taught to slaves, who combined it with African. Our own language is peppered with the same, because some of those African-American women took care of us as we grew up.

I ran to find Grandma, who had gone to the kosher butcher to buy a chicken for that day. In the times long ago, you went to market every day, because you had only the icebox. The kosher butcher was an old man. Not too neat, he wore a very used apron, to put it politely. The chickens were in wooden cages. They were all sticking their heads out between the wooden slats, making noises.

We chose the hen we wanted. The butcher took it out by its feet, and it tried with all its might to get away. Holding on to the legs, putting the head down on a butcher block table covered with newspaper, he took a large knife, and wham, chopped its head off. Then he let it go. It flew to the ground, running around with

> CLANG, CLANG CLANG: So goes the trolley in the words of the song, and so it went through the old City Market, as we've been told after raising the question from Tony Mathews again last week. No less than three Savannahians said they recalled the days when an open-air streetcar rumbled down into the lower level of the market from St. Julian Street and exited up and onto Barnard.
>
> One lady, Helen Cranman, recalled riding the trolley as a tot. "On hot summer days," she said, "it would roll into the welcome cool of the market, where the sound of chickens and the din of commerce could be heard."

Savannah Morning News, *January 15, 1989*

its head off until it dropped dead. Ugh! He chopped off the legs, wrapping everything in newspaper. The feathers still had to be picked off. He wrapped the bird in paper and put it in a knitted bag Grandma had brought with her.

We decided we would walk back. On the way out of the market, we stopped to buy some vegetables. Grandma bought us a bottled Coke which had been sitting in a wash tub full of ice. We shared it on the way back to her house. We passed the fire station, which was near Grandma's, and saw the big fire trucks.

At that time we lived near the big park (Forsyth Park), and could walk there or to other places, like Leopold's, to get ice cream, or downtown to the movies.

Grandma and I got to her house on Barnard Street. We went out on the back porch where she could pluck the feathers off the chicken. She gave me some feathers so I could play with them, to tickle my face and my arms. We talked while she peeled potatoes, carrots, onions, celery, washed the chicken, put them all in a pot, and added water to make soup. She put wood and paper inside the stove to make a fire, so she could put the pot on top to cook. There were no electric or gas stoves until a later time.

Every time I eat chicken soup, I think of my Grandma Anna. She was my mother's mother. She died in our house when she was fifty-four years old, when I was only eight; I still love to think about going to the City Market with her on those special days.

Lord Have Mercy

I was six and my big sister was nine when Momma informed us that our fondest wish was going to come true. We would have a baby sister or brother. We thought Momma was getting fat, but in the 1930s you just didn't discuss such things.

"What do you think it will be?" my sister asked me. "Well, I hope it's not a boy. Boys are such pains. Let's wish for a little sister. Won't that be fun?"

Mother walked into our bedroom at that moment and said "You girls will have to help Lottie with everything for the baby, because I have to work with Daddy at the office."

"We'll help. Just you wait and see." I could hardly wait for the day to come. Momma meant what she said. The two of us were more than willing. Miriam and I just loved the tiny baby clothes. We examined the mounds of cloth diapers; back then that was the only kind to be had. Lottie showed us how to fold them so they would fit a little baby.

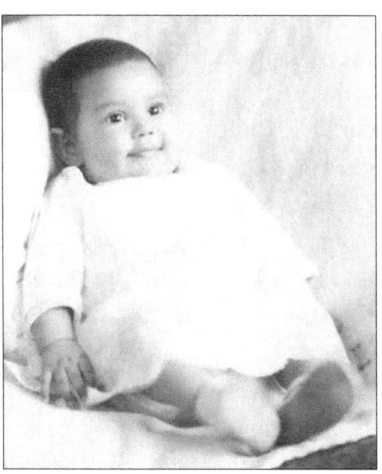

Elinor

Finally the day arrived! On August 18, 1932, our sister was born. She had black hair, dark eyes, and everything about her was round. Her little eyes were round. Her little head was round. She was so chubby that even her little arms were round. Her name was Elinor.

We helped Lottie with the baby as we were supposed to.

Since Elinor slept a lot, we still had time to run outside and play, then dash home, eat lunch, fold diapers, and do other chores. Sometimes Lottie took us to the big park. They had swings, seesaws or balls to play with. Miriam carried her skates. I always ran over Lottie's heels with my tricycle, much to her consternation. A lady at the park taught us how to play all kinds of games or we did our own things. Sometimes we played hopscotch on the cement walkways, because our sidewalks and streets were brick.

One day no one was home but Lottie, Elinor, and me. After folding diapers, I got on the sofa to put my feet up on the Oriental rug which still hung on the wall. Elinor, then three months old, was in the next room asleep in her crib. Suddenly, coming from that room, I heard the sound of paper tearing then a loud bang. The walls shook. There was a big thud, then the sound of a horrible crash. Elinor started screaming. I jumped down, running into the bedroom with Lottie following.

"What have you done? Didn't your Momma tell you to stay off of that wall?"

"I didn't do anything. Look at what happened."

Lottie picked up the shrieking baby, as we looked in horror at the scene before us. A piece of ceiling plaster to which the wallpaper was attached, easily four feet wide and six feet long, broke right over the baby's crib. As we looked at it, the paper came loose; the plaster fell between the crib and the wall. The crib was filled with small pieces of plaster, also all kinds of debris. Lottie tried to comfort Elinor, who had powdered plaster all over her. Lottie was saying, "Lord, have mercy. The haints done tried to kill my baby, but the Lord Almighty done saved her. Thanks, dear G-d, dear Jesus."

She ran to the telephone and dialed the office. "Miss Goldie, the plaster done fell in the bedroom over the baby's crib. You better come quickly. No, ma'am, I don't think she's hurt, but I don't know." Elinor was still screaming at full volume.

Lottie was holding her with me hovering around. We went to the front window to wait for my parents to come home. In about five minutes, Momma came driving the car around the corner on two wheels. Daddy was standing on the running board of the car hanging onto an open window.

They came inside, climbing the steps two at a time. Momma grabbed Elinor, who stopped screaming when she saw Momma.

"That chile woulda been kilt if that plaster had fallen in that crib, but the Lord done saved her today."

"You're absolutely right, Lottie," Momma said "No two ways about it."

Momma looked at Daddy, saying, "We have a perfectly beautiful house out on 45th Street. We moved back downtown because the doctor said it would help Miriam's asthma. It hasn't helped her a bit to be here. Let's move out of this house."

That same day when Miriam came home from spending the night out, I had lots to tell her. All about how Lottie and I saved the baby's life, and how Momma came rushing home with Daddy hanging on to the side of the car and running up the steps to make sure Elinor was all right, which she was.

Grandma and Grandpa Schmalheiser

My grandfather was known as Old Man Schmalheiser. We, however, never referred to him as old, because he never did seem so to us.

Grandpa Philip Schmalheiser

Grandpa had a rhythm to his step. A cute little man, about five-foot-three, with a head full of hair, a round nose, a big bushy mustache, and light eyes. Because of his Russian background, he looked Asian. He came from Austria-Hungary. He called himself Philip, but according to the Ellis Island records, his real name was Raphael.

When my cousins, our friends, and I came to his house, we'd get all wet, because Grandpa would always be outside in the yard watering his flowers with the hose, and as we came up the front walk he would swing around to sprinkle us. We'd go shrieking and scrambling up the steps trying to run away.

Grandpa and Grandma Schmalheiser lived on West Anderson Street. When I was little, Grandma used to rock me in a chair on the front porch, singing a lullaby in Yiddish, which ended with, "Potch her on the tushala." She would then give me a little tap on my rear end (tushy). That's the best memory I have of her. She was always very quiet and good.

Near their house, around the corner on the lane, someone had turned a garage into a confectionary. It was a very tiny edifice that sold cigarettes, chewing tobacco, and all kinds of penny and nickel candy. Sometimes they even had soft drinks to buy. Occasionally

Grandma and Grandpa Schmalheiser

Grandpa would give us each a penny, and we'd race to the store to see what we could get.

What choices we had: Tootsie Rolls, bubble gum, jaw breakers, suckers, plus some other types of candy. There were Milky Ways, Snickers, and Hershey Bars, ice cream or a Coke available, which were five pennies. My favorite candies were little ice cream cones filled with colored marshmallows. You could get three of those for a penny. Then you could eat one, saving the other two. The Coke came in glass bottles, for which there was a refund given if you returned the bottle to the store, probably a penny each.

When the Jewish holidays came, it was a fun time for Grandpa, too. He never went to services, but to please my grandmother, my mother, and my aunt, he participated with vigor in the holidays. He especially liked Passover, as we all did. The smells were so wonderful. The table always sparkled with Grandma's silver and china. Usually we had our grandparents, my momma, daddy, my two sisters and me, my aunt and uncle, with their two daughters.

Grandma Rose Lewis Schmalheiser

We would all be called to the table at sunset on the evening before the first day of Passover, because that is when the holiday starts according to our religion. We took our places. Grandpa always made an impressive entrance last, bathed and shaved (no beard for him, just his mustache), white starched shirt, vest with pants to match. He always had on a tie. He never wore a yarmulke as is the custom, but a grey felt hat with the brim turned down on one side, up on the other, nattily, like the gangster of the twenties in the movies. First he began to pour the wine. That was his job. We didn't pass our glasses to him. He'd jump up from his chair, run around the table filling glasses to the brim. Ours, too.

He'd start the service. I still don't know if he was reading in Hebrew or English, because you couldn't understand his rendition of the service, which went like this: "*Na da da da da daaaaaaaaaaaaa hmmmmmmm, da da na na daaaaaaaaaaaaa, hmmm.*" We'd drink wine, or eat at the times in the service when we were supposed to. Then Grandpa would run around the table filling up all our glasses again. Momma and my Aunt Margie always got so excited, "Papa, Papa, you'll get them all drunk. Please, Papa." His answer was always the same, "It won't hurt them. It's only once a year."

My favorite time of the whole service was when it came time to name the ten plagues. That is when the reader of the service dips his finger into a glass of wine every time he names one of the plagues, until he has named them all. Because Grandpa was a roofing contractor, he always had a cut on at least one of his fingers. This was in the days before Band-Aids, so he always had a gauze bandage on one of them. It was always that finger he dipped in the wine as he counted the ten plagues. It was more or less the end of the Seder for us, because by then we'd all be a little tipsy. We got the giggles, not being able to stop. No matter how much Momma or my aunt fussed, we'd just slide off our chairs under the dining room table, where they couldn't reach us too easily. The Oriental rug was soft and warm. We would fall asleep to the sound of Grandpa's droning voice, "*Na na na, da da da da daaaaaaaaaaaaa hmmmmmmm,*" staying there until Daddy woke us to go home.

Since he was a sporty guy, the first car I remember my Grandpa had was a dark green two-door Model A Ford. The passenger seat folded up under the dash board. He let us push up the seat and get in the car to play house, whenever he wasn't using it. When he was driving it, he drove like a stagecoach with six horses. He didn't stop at stop signs or street lights. He'd whip around corners, *never* missing the curb, much to the discomfort of those riding with him. I never remember Grandma or anyone else in the car, just us poor little granddaughters.

His next car was a dark blue four-door Ford V8. He volunteered to take us to and pick us up from Sunday school. My sisters, my cousins and I were always trying to get someone else to come for us, to no avail.

Grandma and Grandpa Schmalheiser

"Please, Momma. You've never ridden with him. You can drive a car yourself. When I grow up and have children of my own, I'm never going to let them ride with Grandpa."

"I don't think that will be a problem for you." Momma said. "Now get ready. He's coming to take y'all to Sunday school soon."

My big sister was the oldest, so she got to sit in the front seat. The other four of us sat in the back seat, hiding our eyes so we wouldn't see Grandpa speed through stop signs or just miss red lights. He never put his hand out the window to signal which way he was going or turning, since there were no turn signals on cars in the 1930s.

The trip to Sunday school was not nearly as bad as coming home. He would be waiting as we came out of the Sunday school door, five little girls all dressed up, climbing into the car, laughing and giggling as we got in.

We took off down the one-way street called Whitaker, going for several blocks until it dead-ended at Victory Drive, where we made a left turn. Every week as we reached the intersection of Victory Drive and Habersham Street, it would be at the same time as a local streetcar. We'd be going east, the streetcar would be going south, which meant someone had to cross the spot first or there would be a very big smash-up.

"Papa," we'd scream, "Stop! Stop! The streetcar will hit us."

Grandpa went right on. It wasn't because he didn't hear us. We hugged each other, covering our faces, falling off the seat to the floor so we wouldn't have to see the mayhem about to occur. We shut our eyes as he accelerated, beating the street car to the intersection.

As there was no air conditioning in the car, all the windows were open and in the streetcar, too.

The conductor clanged his bell. It was a warning for us to get out of the way. He was always expecting us. As we roared past, just missing each other, he'd yell out, "Hey, Mr. Schmalheiser, how y'all doin', girls? Fine, I hope," waving, smiling as we bumped over the streetcar tracks, bouncing and screaming. Grandpa waved. We raised our heads and hands, waving too.

Needless to say, the rest of the trip was pretty quiet. That night I thanked G-d for saving me for another week.

My grandpa dropped dead at eighty-five, running to answer the telephone.

Grandma and Grandpa Schmalheiser's house on West Anderson Street

Grandpa's Bathtub

Perhaps it doesn't sound very important today, because all of us in this country take our bathtubs for granted. Think of all the "boat people" who emigrated here, who never had a bathtub or hadn't even seen a toilet. When the country of Israel airlifted 40,325 Ethiopians to Israel, the thing that fascinated those people the most, when they got there, was taking a bath or flushing the toilet.

In the 1990s, I was invited by a film producer to the meeting of an oral history group for the making of a documentary film being funded by a federal grant. This was to video-record some of the stories from the past told by people in the Savannah Jewish Community.

The gathered group was so excited to see each other, recalling all the wonderful times or the not so wonderful times we had as children. We were also going to tell some of the stories told to us by our parents and grandparents. It would take us back to the early 1900s or before. The film would be for our children, grandchildren, and great grandchildren, about the history of our local Jewish people.

One gentleman of advanced age told the story of taking a bath every Saturday night. That's right, only once a week for the people who lived in a downtown area known as Yamacraw Village. Not the greatest area, but they did not consider themselves

#2 *washtub*

poor, preferring that certain area because they needed to be within walking distance of the synagogue, since they were all Jewish. Most of the parents were immigrants, but the children were born in this country.

My friend Harry told about taking a bath on Saturday night in a #2 washtub. Since there were no washing machines, people had to wash their clothes in these large round tubs made out of galvanized steel, using a washboard to scrub the clothes. The tub was brought into the kitchen once a week for everyone to use. That sounds simple enough.

Taking a bath in the tub in the middle of the kitchen must have been very difficult, Harry said. If they had running water inside, they still had to use buckets to fill up the tub. Hot water heaters didn't come out for a few more years. Until then they had to heat the water on a wood stove. After the tub was filled, the family started to bathe: the grandparents, the mama, the papa, the children, (maybe there were ten of them.) Getting the idea? Maybe the girls went first, but who knew. Did they change the water? Harry didn't say. After he told his story, I stood up to be recognized.

My grandparents, my father, his two brothers and four sisters lived in a large two-story house. Grandpa decided "enough" of the #2 washtub. He would take a corner area in their house to make a real bathtub. He built some sort of shape (of wood, I guess), for a tub, lining it with metal. Through the wall of the tub to the outside, he put a pipe. The pipe was stopped up with a cloth to keep the water from running out. After it was filled with the heated water, everyone took their baths, then they pulled out the cloth. The water ran out, going to the ground outside the house. *Voila!* Indoor plumbing had arrived on Zubly Street. My father's family had the first bathtub on their street.

"That's right, they did!" my friend Harry echoed.

Floradora and My Great Aunt

This is a story about my great Aunt Flora who lived with us when I was six and shared a bedroom and a double bed with me in 1931.

One of the first musicals of note on the English stage and then Broadway was *Floradora*. It had already had a run of more than four hundred performances in London when it opened in New York in November 1900. At first there was no indication that it would be much of a success. However, a song we still remember, "Tell Me, Pretty Maiden," was sung by a group of six girls who became known as The Floradora Sextet. It was they who began attracting theater-goers. Some reviews call them "the most beautiful women on the stage." Men lavished gifts on these young ladies, and would come night after night, buying seats down front to get close to the girls, who would smile, wink, and flirt with them.

The original sextet was composed of Margaret Walker, Daisy Green, Marjorie Relyea, Vaughn Texsmith, Marie Wilson, and Agnes Wayburn, but some of them either married or found wealthy admirers, so the cast of six kept changing. Lots of girls came and left. I cannot believe it, but my grandmother's sister was one of them. Her name was Belle Fisher, but she was called Flora. I can't find out a great deal of information, but as time goes on more information seems to appear on the Internet.

This is my story as I remember her:

"I'll race you to the top of the stairs," Aunt Flora challenged me, as she leaned heavily on her two canes. I looked up at her. I knew that it was dangerous for her to try to race up the stairs, but I wouldn't hurt her feelings, so I said, "Bet I can beat you."

"Bet you can't," she answered.

Just at that moment Momma leaned over the bannister, looking down the stairwell, and asked in her strictest voice, "Aunt Flora, what are you two doing?"

Aunt Flora winked at me; "We're just having a race to the top of the stairs."

"You'll fall!" Heaving a big sigh, Momma moved away, going into the apartment. She knew it was hopeless to try to tell either one of us anything.

There I was, a feisty little girl, standing beside a very portly elderly lady, who was bent over from arthritis. She had such badly crippled feet that she leaned heavily on two walking canes. She was my grandmother's sister. As we looked at each other, we knew we were soul mates.

"When I say, ready, set, go, we'll start, "Aunt Flora said.

"All right," I said, crouching down into what I thought looked like a racing position.

Aunt Flora straightened up as best she could, then making herself ready, she said,

"Ready, set, go!"

I flew up the stairs as Aunt Flora struggled with her feet, her canes, and her back, huffing and puffing all the way. As I got to the landing, I glanced back to see how much I was winning. Then I pretended to trip so I would fall. Aunt Flora caught up with me; we finished at the top of the stairs, neck and neck.

As we walked into the apartment, I said, "Aunt Flora, you promised to tell me about when you went to see the king."

"Let's set the table for supper. I'll tell you after we eat."

"Oh boy, you're really going to tell me. I can hardly wait."

We went into the dining room, got the silver, the dishes, and the glassware,

Aunt Flora

setting the table for supper. I knew just where all the silver, glasses, and dishes went. My mother taught me. Aunt Flora had taught her.

Aunt Flora had lived in New York City all her life. She had come to the deepest part of the South for a while. I had seen her once or twice in New York when we went to visit Grandma and Grandpa, but when she came to stay, I took to her right away. Aunt Flora thought I looked just like her. She said her hair was straight and brown just like mine even when she was young. She wore it long, twisting it into a bun, as all older ladies did in those days.

With supper eaten, dishes put away, it was time for me to get ready for bed. Aunt Flora and I took turns in the bathroom, putting on our pajamas, washing our faces, brushing our teeth. Then we

Aunt Flora

went into our bedroom, where Aunt Flora slept in the bed with me. She took the pins from her hair, brushing it one hundred times or more. As she did, she started to tell me her story.

"Well, you see, I was a dancer and singer on the stage in New York City. We danced in lots of other places too. We were called The Floradora Girls. There were only six of us at one time."

"Ooooh," I breathed. "You must have been so beautiful."

"Well, I don't know about that, but I was thinner and had a good figure," she went on.

Then she straightened up, held her head up high. For a moment she looked twenty again. She was so very beautiful. She looked in the mirror to see her reflection, sighing.

Turning to me, she asked, "Do you remember how long it takes you to go to New York from Savannah on the boat?"

"Yes."

"Well, it took a lot longer to go by boat to England. That's where the king lived. I went to see him."

"Really," I said, as I sat on my bed, fascinated. She looked at me, silently laughing at my look of wonder.

"The king was called 'Bertie,' but his title was 'The Prince of Wales.' He was the son of Queen Victoria. He became King Edward VII. He's still the king today."

I had so many questions to ask. "Why did they call him 'Bertie' and Prince whatever. Was his mother a queen like Cinderella?"

"Yes, his mother was a queen just like Cinderella. She even had a gold coach."

"Wow!"

Edward VII
King Edward after his coronation in 1902, painted by Sir Luke Fildes, National Portrait Gallery, London

"His real name was Edward Albert Christian George Andrew Patrick David. He had seven names. His title was the Prince of Wales, but everyone called him 'Bertie', taken from Albert."

"What's a title?"

"Prince, king, queen. Like that," Aunt Flora answered while she brushed her hair and tied it back with a shoe string.

"Now I understand."

"His mother was the queen for sixty years. He was the oldest son. He was the person next in line to become the head of his country. They didn't do like we do here and vote for president. He just got to be king because he was the oldest in his family," she told me.

"I won't get to be the queen in this family, will I?"

"No, sweetie, you don't stand a chance," she patted me on the shoulder, giving me a hug.

FLORADORA AND MY GREAT AUNT

"Bertie liked all the ladies, especially The Floradora Girls," she continued. "He didn't think he'd ever become king, since his mother was the queen for sixty years. She had to die for him to become king."

"I'm sure he didn't want his mother to die," I said.

"I'm sure he didn't," Aunt Flora answered. "He told us, if he ever became king, he would invite us all to the coronation, which is exactly what he did."

"What's a coronation?" I'd never heard of that before.

"That's when they crown the king. Suppose I tell you all about it, then you will understand." I nodded my head in agreement.

"I bought all my clothes for the occasion," Aunt Flora said. "In those days you didn't go into a store to buy a dress. You had to go to a lady who made dresses, pick out a picture of a dress or dresses you liked. She took all your measurements, so she could make your dresses. You had to go back to her to get them fitted. It was a big long process. I got all my dresses made. I had to have hats and gloves made to match. Stockings and shoes were also needed."

I could feel my eyes widen in wonder as she talked. "You must have been very rich then to buy all that."

Aunt Flora just looked at me at me, laughing, saying, "Yes, I was then. I had twelve suitcases. It took many days and weeks to get ready. Finally the day came to go to England. We filled the carriage with our luggage, before we went down to the boat."

"Like the boat we take to New York?" I was well traveled.

"Yes, just like that, only larger."

"We got on the boat and were taken to the staterooms that Prince Edward had arranged for us. After a lovely but long trip across the ocean, we arrived in London. The day we arrived it was very foggy, even though it was August. Carriages met us at the boat, ordered by His Majesty. That's another name they called Prince Albert, Bertie, Prince of Wales, soon to be King Edward the VII.

"We had several days as His Majesty's guests. Sightseeing, getting our clothes ready, being given invitations to the coronation, the coronation ball, all kinds of parties. We were also given instructions as to where and when we would be picked up, because we were to ride in the coronation parade."

"A parade, you rode in a real parade, Aunt Flora?"

"Oh, yes. You know the picture you have of me standing in front of the carriage?"

"Yes, yes. Is that the carriage you rode in?"

"The very one, with the dress I wore to the coronation, but I wore a different dress when I was presented at court. I went to the coronation ball at Buckingham Palace."

I sighed, a real palace, just like in Cinderella.

Aunt Flora and the coronation parade carriage

"So, then," Aunt Flora went on, "when our carriage came for us, it was all covered with roses."

"Just like in the picture," I said.

"That's right. That picture was taken in the courtyard of Buckingham Palace. Bertie and his family rode in carriages, gold ones, much more beautiful than the one the Fairy G-dmother made for Cinderella."

"It was more beautiful than that? Oh, I wish I could have seen it."

Aunt Flora finished putting hand cream on her hands. "Well, maybe one day you can go to England to see them."

I jumped up and down on the bed. "You really think so? Tell me the rest."

FLORADORA AND MY GREAT AUNT

"We rode slowly from the palace to Westminster Abbey. That is the church where all the English kings and queens are crowned. That day was August 9th, 1902. There were lots of soldiers marching and riding on horseback in the parade. The streets were decorated with beautiful flags and streamers flying in the air, hanging from buildings and poles. We waved to the people who stood on the sidewalk cheering. It was thrilling! The bobbies (that is their police) had to hold them back.

Prince Albert's golden coach

"We arrived at the church and took our seats, preparing to wait for the Prince of Wales who would become the new king. Beautiful church music was being played on the organ.

"Many kings, queens, princes, and princesses came. They were very beautifully dressed with jewelry all over them. The men were in spectacular uniforms. Flowers were everywhere. All the guests were already seated when we walked in. The royal family came down the aisle, taking their seats at the front of the church.

"Then Prince Edward came. He had a long purple robe trimmed in white fur over his formal uniform. He walked down the very long aisle to the altar. As he stood there, the ministers took off his robe and introduced him to all the people in the church. Of course, everyone knew who he was, but that's part of the ceremony. Then Prince Edward sat on the throne where the ceremony of crowning took place. The Archbishop of Canterbury, their minister, put drops of oil on his head. The service of crowning is a religious one done by the ministers. Next the Archbishop gave him the scepter and the orb."

"What is that?" I interrupted; because I was so excited, I didn't say excuse me. Momma had asked Aunt Flora to take me in hand, to try to make a lady out of me, as she had done for my mother when she was my age.

She continued, "The scepter is a long pole with diamonds. The orb is a round ball with diamonds on it, with a cross on the top. After that they put this very special crown on his head. Spectacular is the only word to describe his crown. It had diamonds with all kinds of huge stones all over it.

"Then they declared him the king of the whole British Empire, which includes lots of countries. They also had a ceremony to crown his wife, the queen. Both ceremonies were more beautiful than anything else I have ever seen. Afterward we rode the carriages back to the palace where we had lunch. When we finished, we were taken back to our hotel so we could rest, then get dressed for dinner to attend the Coronation Ball."

This was better than Cinderella. We even had pictures of Aunt Flora from the Coronation Parade.

"Was he a king like King David and King Solomon?" Since I was a little Jewish girl, those were the kings I knew about.

"Well, yes, sort of that way. The purple robe and the lions you see on things that belong to the English royal family were taken from the royal families of Israel. Purple was their royal color. The lions come from the Lion of Judah."

I did not understand what she meant, but in later years I realized the meaning.

She continued, "That evening we were all dressed in beautiful ball gowns."

"Ball gowns like the Fairy G-dmother gave to Cinderella?"

Aunt Flora laughed, "Yes, just like that. We went to Buckingham Palace, where we had dinner. Afterward, we were presented at Court."

"What is presented at Court?"

"Well, the king and queen sat on thrones in a large room. A long carpet leads up to the throne. A man announced our names to the king. Announces means he says your name very loud. You walk up the carpet to where they are sitting. When you get there, you curtsy to the floor."

FLORADORA AND MY GREAT AUNT

"What is a curtsy?"

Aunt Flora stood up. Holding onto the foot of the bed, she put one leg behind her, gracefully bending the other knee and bowing her head.

"We had to be taught how to do it perfectly. So I bowed to the king and queen."

"The queen, too?"

"Oh, yes."

"Ooooh, was she very beautiful?"

"Yes, yes, she was. She had on a beautiful dress with beads all over it. The king had on a beautiful uniform. They both wore their crowns. Then we had to back up along the carpet, because you didn't turn your back to the king and queen. After that we went to a ballroom in the palace where we ate first, spending almost all night dancing. Afterward the carriages came to take us back to our hotel."

"Just like Cinderella?"

"Yes, just like Cinderella."

"Did you meet Prince Charming?"

"Well, I did meet some princes."

"Did you dance with them?"

"Yes, I did."

"Did any of them want to marry you?

She laughed out loud, "Oh no."

"Are you married, Aunt Flora?"

"No, I've never been married."

"Aunt Flora, you don't even have any children."

"No," she answered softly.

"But why don't you?" I insisted.

"I was going to be married to a very wonderful man. I went to Europe—Paris, France, to be exact. That is right near England. I went to buy my trousseau."

"What is a trousseau?"

"It's a French word. It means a wedding dress, a veil, shoes, stockings, underwear, nightgowns, and lots of other things. All the things you might need for getting married."

"You got all new things?" I asked. I was a person who wore her sister's hand-me-downs.

"Yes, all new. Then while I was gone, my fiancé caught the grippe and died."

"What is a fiancé and what is the grippe?" So many new words were hard for me to learn.

"*Fiancé* is another French word. It means the person you are engaged to marry. Grippe is an illness like a very bad cold."

"You must have been very upset"

"Yes, very sad." Sadness filled her voice. With that she just said, "It's really time to go to sleep."

We hugged each other. I told her I loved her; she told me, too. After that night we had many lovely days together. Then after a few months had gone by, it was time for her to go back to New York, which she sorely missed.

When she got back to New York, she sent us all kinds of things, jewelry, fur stoles. To me she sent the dark glasses she wore in the coronation parade and some stockings and gloves from her trousseau.

I asked Momma why she never married. Momma said she loved her fiancé very much. He was her only love. After he died she lived in her brownstone house with the butler, maid, and cook. When Momma was a little girl, Aunt Flora used to send for Mother to come to her house to spend the weekends. She had a long banquet table in her dining room; she sat at one end with Momma sitting at the other. The butler served them. Sometimes there were guests. She taught Momma manners, bought her clothes and even a beautiful doll. She lived like that until she had to sell her house and furniture. That was because her money ran out. She was too old to be a Floradora Girl. There weren't any more, anyway.

In Aunt Flora's last years, Momma and Aunt Charlotte (Momma's sister) took care of her. Aunt Charlotte used go to New York on buying trips for her store in North Carolina, and she would go to see Aunt Flora.

I never saw her again. A few years later she died.

They buried her at the Mount Hope Cemetery in New York.

Floradora and My Great Aunt

It was not until she died that I found out her real name was Belle Fisher. They put *Belle Flora Fisher* on her grave stone. She would have liked that.

The Bi-lo Baby

One summer day in Savannah, an eight-year-old Henny put on her boy's overalls and sneakers. She combed her straight brown hair, and then ran outside with their dog, Bozo, who was a small Boston terrier. He was black with a white blaze running between his eyes, having the saddest expression on his face.

Henny was in too much of a hurry to see what the other girls were doing. She made up her mind to play by herself. Hilda, the Great Dane, who lived next door, was faithfully waiting for them by the garage. Henny drew a hopscotch on the paved driveway, jumping as the dogs watched

The other three girls, Mimi (her big sister), Arne (her baby sister), and Cousin Regina were dressed in their hand-smocked white starched dresses; they had on Mary Jane shoes and ribbons in their curly red hair. (Except Baby Sister, who had curly black hair.) They all went on the front stoop to play house.

Mimi smoothed the front of her lovely dress. Turning to Baby Sister, she said, "Go find Bozo. We need him so we can put the baby cap on him, and put him in the carriage, and then we'll have another baby besides Regina's doll baby. What's her name, anyway, Regina? Just Baby, okay. But Bozo will have to have a name. He can't be a baby called Bozo. We'll think of something," she said with an air of importance

Arne said, "What about me?"

THE BI-LO BABY

"Oh, well." Regina sighed at having to play with a four-year-old and a dog. She was our older cousin from Atlanta. "Why don't you be a baby sister?" Regina answered.

Baby Sister smiled and put her thumb in her mouth, saying, "Ga, ga, goo, goo."

"Go get the dog," hissed Mimi. "Don't bring Henny or Hilda. They can't play with us."

Baby Sister went around the side of the house. She tried to pick Bozo up, but he didn't want to go, slithering out of her arms like a snake. He was happy where he was.

Hilda the Great Dane growled at her.

Henny stopped hopping and turned around to Baby Sister to say, "Go away. Leave us alone."

Baby Sister stubbornly stood her ground. "Mimi told me to get Bozo, so he can be the baby in the carriage. We're playing house on the front steps, but you can't play."

As she talked, she combed her fingers through her black curls and smoothed down the front of her white dress, now a little smudged and dirty from drooling when she sucked her thumb.

Henny stood there with her straight brown hair, overalls, and sneakers. "I want to play," she announced.

Baby Sister avoided looking at her. There was a long silence.

"Can't I please come and play?" begged Henny.

"I don't think so," was the answer."

"Well, then, you can't have Bozo. Stay here, Bo."

The dogs gave Baby Sister a bored but defiant look.

"Well, come on; ask her yourself," suggested Baby Sister.

"I'm not going to. She told me just to get Bozo, you and Hilda can't come. That's what she said."

Henny, Hilda and Bozo went to the corner of the house. They peeked around to see what was going on, not daring to show themselves all at once.

73

Out of the corner of her eye, Mimi noticed Henny and the two dogs. Drawing herself up haughtily, she spoke, "Bozo, get over here right now! Get in the carriage under the cover. Let Baby Sister put the cap on your head. I mean this minute!"

She could really be bossy. She sounded just like Momma. Bozo, recognizing the voice of authority, deserted Henny. He hopped up into the carriage and let Baby Sister put the cap on his head. Then, he lay on his back as the baby blanket was put over his stomach and his paws hung out. He played the part with resignation. Hilda came over, looked at him, and sniffed a little, and walked disgustedly away.

Henny, forgetting her resolve to remain aloof, came running out. "Please let me play, Mimi. Can't I, Regina? Please. Oh, please."

Mimi gave a sigh. "You can play house with us, but only if you be the daddy and don't touch the babies." "Why?" asked Henny. "Daddies hold babies. They give them the bottle, too."

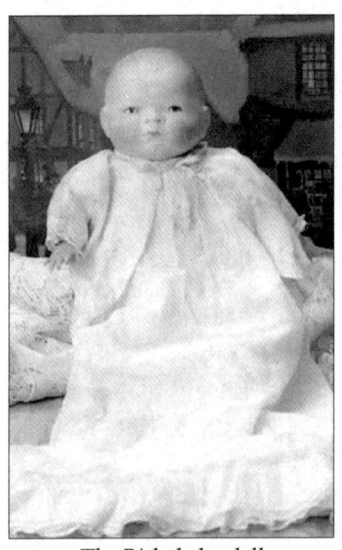

The Bi-lo baby doll

Mimi answered "Because you have on overalls and sneakers. Regina is the grandmother; I'm the mother, Baby Sister, Bozo, and the Bi-lo Baby are the babies. We have enough mommas to take care of them."

Henny fumed. It was so hot, but Momma made her wear overalls, which none of the others did. She just liked to climb trees, jump off the garage with the boys. She got her knees so dirty, Momma had to clean them with Bon Ami cleanser. Then Momma would comb her hair in little corkscrew curls, going to great pains, taking forever to do so.

The Bi-lo Baby

Looking at her, Momma said, "You'll wear overalls during the week, so your knees will clean for Sunday school." Henny missed Momma fussing over her, but she didn't miss the dresses or the curls. However, at that moment, when she wanted to play house, she had regrets about jumping off the garage. The other three girls did look nice with their dresses, shoes, and beautiful hair that tumbled down over their shoulders.

Bozo was staying in the baby carriage. He had now turned traitor, enjoying every minute, because he knew they were going to give him a bottle with a nipple on it to get him to stay.

The doll was lying on a pillow on the floor of the front porch. Mimi and Regina were hovering over it. Baby Sister was still standing there sucking her thumb.

Willing to be the daddy with the hope that perhaps they would let her hold the doll, Henny edged over closer to them. Lying there on a pillow, the doll looked so real with its white bisque head; those blue eyes that opened and closed. The body was soft; it felt human when you held it. It cried when you turned it over, like a real baby.

A maternal longing suddenly surfaced, overtaking Henny. It could only be satisfied by the feel of the doll's body next to her bosom. She wanted to rock it back and forth. Even sing to it.

"I just want to hold the baby doll for a minute. Pleeeease, Mimi."

"No, I told you. That's it." Henny stood on one foot, then the other. Edging closer and closer, she couldn't even get a good look at it. Mimi said, "You smell sweaty, move."

Henny couldn't stand it another minute. Fury overtook her. She took a quick step. Sweeping over, she reached across the girls, making a grab for the doll.

She missed! She grabbed the pillow, instead! It happened so fast she didn't realize what she had done until she saw the doll flying across the porch, landing on the brick steps. It made a loud crash, smashing its head to bits. She dropped the pillow. There was a stunned silence. Then tears rolled down onto the girls' beautiful dresses, now soiled. They began screaming, then jumping up and down.

"Look at what you've done. It's Regina's doll. Momma's gonna give it to you. You're really gonna get it now! You'll be spanked and punished for at least a year!" As Mimi yelled at Henny, she and Regina continued to sob, rubbing their eyes.

"Ooooh, what are we going to do?" Mimi kept saying.

Baby Sister's eyes got wide with fear. She sucked her thumb openly now. Bozo jumped out of the carriage and ran down the street with the lace baby cap on his head and the cover dragging behind him. Hilda the Great Dane followed close behind.

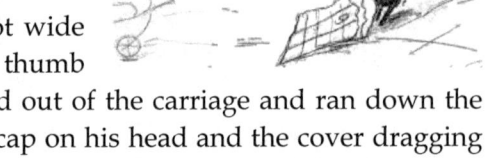

What did Henny do? You might ask. She just turned on her heels, without a tear, but in real shock. The precious baby laid inert, no longer looking real, but just a doll with about a hundred pieces where the beautiful head had been. An eye rolled down the steps. They stared at it. It stared back.

As Henny walked away, she began singing, "I don't care, I don't care, what you may think of me," but inside, her little heart was breaking and as long as she lived, she would never get over what she had done.

Henny is what I used to call myself, and she is really *me*.

Tybee Tales

Riding the Train to Tybee

Every summer many people left the city because it became so unbearably hot and humid. In most houses there was no cross ventilation; the fans were useless. We had to go somewhere to cool off. Tybee Island, about twenty miles away, was the perfect spot. We could always find a place at the beach, where the air was cooler, the water was there for swimming, and life in general was very simple, but lots of fun.

One of my fondest memories about those years was the train ride to Tybee. A road had been built, but the train, which was the original transportation, was still running. We loved to ride it to the beach. We didn't get to ride the train anyplace else, so this was an experience.

Photo courtesy of Tybee Island Historical Society

It was Miriam's and my job to pack clothes for Elinor and the two of us. Lottie supervised everything. Wee Tong ran around, all excited, as though he knew something was going on. We had to fill up the car with all our belongings. Afterward Mother would take Lottie, Miriam, Elinor, and me down to the train station to ride to the beach. Then she went back to the house, where Daddy helped her load the car with whatever else we needed for the summer.

Wee Tong got in the back of the car, with the window rolled down enough so he could stick his head out to catch the breeze, barking at everything he saw.

Lottie bought our tickets, and we sat in the station waiting until the conductor came by calling, "All aboard." The two of us climbed up the steps and went running to sit on seats by the window. They could be arranged facing each other. Miriam sat on one seat, with me on the other. Lottie sat with us on the aisle side holding Baby Elinor. Of course, there was no air conditioning, so the windows on the train were wide open. A fireman had to stoke the engine on the train with coal, because it was a steam engine. The smoke from this fire caused black soot to fly in through the window. It got all over us.

Lottie implored us to close the window, but we knew Momma would be driving by the train, with the dog looking out of the car. Since the road to Tybee paralleled the train tracks, we wanted to yell at them. I remember our great excitement as we pulled out of the station. We were on our way with our heads out of the window waiting for Momma to show up.

Lottie looked at us. "Y'all are gonna fall out. What will I tell your momma?" She hung on to Elinor, now crying because of the noise made by the train. We tried to distract the baby, "Look, Elinor, Momma's coming by in the car. We can wave at her."

Sure enough, along came our car with the dog barking out the back window. "That really is Momma, Lottie, let Elinor look." Lottie brought her over to the window. "Let's wave at Momma and Wee Tong," We yelled at them, leaning out the train window. The dog saw us and barked at the train. Momma just kept looking ahead. She kept on driving, with nary so much as a look or a smile.

"Now you've seen your momma and the dog. Git y'all's heads back in this train. Please shut that window." We didn't do what she told us, hanging out the window and yelling at every car we saw. Daddy went by driving his truck. We yelled at him. He saw us waving, and waved back at us.

"He saw us, Lottie. He waved."

"Wonderful," she said, "Now y'all better behave or I'll have ta tell ya momma how y'all acted." The baby was given a bottle and had fallen asleep.

The ride was soon over and we were at the little train station at the beach. We got off the train, Lottie with the sleeping baby on her shoulder. We walked to the house, about two blocks away. When we got there, Momma and Daddy were still unloading the car and truck. Wee Tong was going around the yard lifting his leg on every bush, marking his territory.

"I see the baby has given out," Momma said

"Yes, ma'am," Lottie answered.

"Did the girls behave?"

Lottie cut her eyes toward us, with a look that said, "You'll be good the whole summer or else you'll be in big trouble."

Then she turned to Momma with a smile, saying, "Yaas'm."

The Iceman, the Vegetable Man, the Fish Lady, and the Milkman

Many people today are not old enough to remember when there were no electrical refrigerators. What we had in those days was called the "icebox." It was made of wood, in various shapes and sizes. Ours had three doors on the front, two short ones on one side and one tall one on the other side. The bottom left side was where we kept a large block of ice.

The ice company gave everyone a large card, which had 25, 50, 75 and 100 printed on the perimeter. This was kept in a front window with the number of pounds of ice you wanted turned up to the top, so you could get that size of ice from the ice man, who came every day.

Inside the icebox on the left side over the ice, we kept things that really needed to be kept cold, like butter or bottles of milk and a large container of water for a cool drink. You could use an ice pick to chip off some slivers to put in a drink. In the top compartments we kept things like meat, lettuce, tomatoes, and fruit; just whatever would go bad in the heat.

Of course, there was no freezer, so you couldn't keep ice cream there. It would melt right away. We had to put a pan on the floor under the ice compartment to catch the water as the ice melted, and then we had to empty the pan.

The ice man's wagon had sides, with a top to keep the sun off, so it would not melt too quickly.

The Iceman, the Vegetable Man

The ice in the wagon was sitting on what looked like hay. It was in huge blocks, covered with burlap. When the ice man saw how much you wanted by looking at the card in the window, he would take his ice pick, neatly chip the ice to the exact amount. He had a huge pair of tongs that hooked into the ice which he put into a large canvas bag. It dripped water all through the house to the icebox.

His horse, who pulled the wagon, knew exactly where to stop. The ice man never had to tell him. The horse would just amble on down to the next place. In summer, when we played outside, the ice man was the highlight of our day. He let us climb on the back step of the wagon to get slivers of ice that fell on the floor. We would hang on, so we could have a ride when the horse walked to the next stop. We were not allowed to pet or talk to him, because he was working, as any distraction would keep him from doing a good job.

There were other vendors who came to the neighborhood. Before dawn every day, the milkman came in a horse-drawn wagon that had rubber wheels, because it made less noise and would not wake people up early in the morning. We left a note every night on the back step to show how much milk we wanted.

There also was a woman who pushed a small cart while balancing a basket on her head. As she walked down the street, she yelled, "Get your oystas and swimp h'yar." If you wanted some, you stopped her and bought them. No one ever wondered when they had been caught. We just knew they were fresh.

In later years, the vegetable man came. He drove a truck. He had fresh corn, snap beans, and all kinds of wonderful things. He always gave us carrots to chew on while our mothers bought vegetables and fruit from him. He came to the beach in the summer with wonderful watermelons, cantaloupe, oranges, and tangerines. There was a store where the post office was. You could get staples, but the grocery store came later, so we depended on the vegetable man and his truck.

The Tybrisa Pavilion

Summers at Tybee were great. In the mornings we went to the beach, taking Elinor with us. She was about a year old. Miriam and I took turns watching her at the water's edge, until one of the adults came to take her home in the stroller, for her lunch and a nap. Imagine, two little girls at the ocean's edge taking care of the baby and being very responsible

We came home around mid-day, took our showers, had lunch, and stayed home during the heat of the day, reading books or listening to the radio. The soap operas were the best. We loved to play board games, mostly Monopoly.

Tybrisa Pavilion in the background

Around three o'clock we'd put on our shoes and go back outside. Shoes were necessary so the hot asphalt on the paved streets would not burn the skin off the bottom of our feet. We ran out of the house, going down the steps yelling, "We'll be at the beach," which was several blocks away. We had the complete run of the island and could go unsupervised. That was over eighty years ago.

One of my most favorite things was to go up on the Pavilion. It was the main focus of the island at the end of the most important street. Its entrance was from the boardwalk, extending out over the beach and ocean about seventy-five yards. In the middle was a dance floor, all polished and shiny with a mirrored ball hanging above that turned at night, sparkling on the floor, when people danced to the music. Around its perimeter were rocking chairs for people to sit, enjoying the ocean, while catching the breezes.

It was the Big Band era. They were the large, fabulous dance bands, playing songs written by Johnny Mercer, Cole Porter, George and Ira Gershwin, and many others. It was a very romantic time. Some of the big bands who came were Tommy Dorsey, Jimmy Dorsey, Bob Crosby, Woody Herman, Benny Goodman, Cab Calloway, Red Nichols, and Ray Teal. It has always amazed me that such famous performers came to Tybee! It was on their way south for winter or to the north in the summer.

In the afternoons the musicians practiced the songs they were going to play for the dancers at night. We were not allowed there during the day, but because I was so little, I would sneak through the metal gate (which was locked) and stretch out on the dance floor, feeling the breezes and listening to their rehearsals all afternoon. That is why today I can hear one line from any of those old songs sung in the thirties and forties, recognize it, and sing all the words.

One night a week they would have amateur hour. I remember once I sang with Bob Crosby's orchestra (Bing's brother); I don't remember what I sang, but I loved doing it. That was my fifteen minutes of fame.

Topless in Tybee

Do you remember when men wore tops to their bathing suits? If you do, you're really old. You don't? Well, I guess it was in the mid-thirties. It was not considered respectable for men to go bare-chested.

At the beach in Savannah, we had a police chief called "High Pockets," who rode his motorcycle all over the island keeping order. He made sure all laws were kept and that men were wearing tops with their bathing trunks.

One summer my older sister's crowd was on the beach when one of their male friends, named Kearthur, whom we called "K," arrived. He had on his bathing trunks, but for the required top he had on a leather belt, which he was wearing diagonally across his chest. Everyone on the beach was shocked. No one had even thought of doing such a thing, much less carrying out such a terrible deed. We all looked at him in horror.

Joseph Schmalheiser and Gus Lipsitz

"K, you are going to get in bad trouble," someone said. All the girls agreed, but the boys just laughed. He sat stubbornly on the beach deciding to be the test case. He was the only person who had such guts. He'd been to Miami. Everyone there went without tops.

We sat together in front of the main parking lot, near the closet-size police station. Sure enough, someone ratted on him, and in short order he was arrested by High Pockets, then taken to jail.

The police station was small, the jail wasn't much larger. Nobody ever stayed there longer than a couple of hours or overnight. That was the caliber of crime at the beach in those days. This was the first crime of this kind, however. We weren't too concerned, but we all rode our bikes to visit him, taking him food and water. He got out the next morning.

The Tybee courthouse, 1940

That was not the end of the incident. K was given a summons to appear before the judge when court was held at the beach a couple of times a year. The courthouse was an old ramshackle wooden building. The steps up to the door were falling down; the paint had long ago peeled off. There were decaying doors and shutters for windows. All of them were opened, to create air. One light bulb hung on a cord, over a desk. When he walked in, the judge faced rows of gray unpainted benches made of old planks. They did have backs, but sitting was difficult because there were plenty of splinters.

The day of the trial arrived. High Pockets and his deputy arrived to open up the courthouse for the waiting crowd. There were a few cases of people being drunk, drunk driving, sleeping on the beach, or theft of cold drinks from the ice chest at the market, and Kearthur's not wearing a bathing suit top.

We all filed in, some people wearing dresses while others wore shorts. People had shoes or bare feet. There were men in bathing suits with tops. Soon the room was filled. Some sat on the window sills, and some hung through the windows from the outside. I was about twelve at the time. I was standing up when the chief announced the judge was coming. Then, looking straight at me, he said anyone not having a seat had to leave. I got so scared thinking, "Can you get arrested for that?" There weren't any more seats. My sister's friend, Buddy, suddenly pulled me down on his lap and the trials began. All the other cases were heard. The last case was K's belt trick. We waited. The judge looked at him.

"I ought to fine you." Everyone in the court room held their breath, waiting to see what would happen.

The judge gave him a lecture for indecent behavior and exposure. K stood there nodding as if he really thought the judge was right.

"Will you wear your bathing suit top or an undershirt in the future, young man?"

K said, "Yes, sir. Yes, sir," not meaning a word of it, as he looked the judge right in the eye.

"All right, Kearthur, as punishment you'll have to ride the garbage truck for two months helping the garbage man."

He would be in the heat and the rain, but at least he didn't have to pay a fine.

"Yea!" we all screamed.

"Order in the court!" High Pockets yelled with a stern face, but he had a twinkle in his eye. That was the beginning of men going topless at our beach.

After that, all the men, including my daddy, quit wearing their old bathing suits with tops. The police would have had to arrest hundreds of men. That just shows how one small act can become a momentous occasion.

Hollywood

Packing Up – California, Here We Come

Daddy put roofs on houses and commercial property in Savannah. When World War II came, he just couldn't get materials or labor, unless he had a government contract, so he went to work at the shipyard, which was building Liberty ships for the war. One day he got hurt working on a ship, and the doctor told him, no more of that kind of work for him.

Daddy decided a trip to California would be a good idea and just what he needed. He could recover, think about what he wanted to do for the rest of his life while taking a nice vacation. So off he went to visit the family and see the beautiful West.

I loved Savannah, thinking I would certainly spend my life here. Little did I dream that Daddy would visit L.A. and then flabbergast us by calling to say he had decided to stay in California. Just like that. He told us he hoped we didn't mind if he didn't return. He was going to work for his brother at the movie studio in Hollywood. All we had to do was to take care of a few minor chores. Soon we could join him. Well, that sounded reasonable; not at all complicated. We would learn!

Since Miriam, my older sister, was off in Alabama with her husband at an Army base, I was next in command to Mother. I was eighteen at the time, attending college in Savannah, planning to become a nurse. Mother, realizing I would have fainted at the first sight of blood, talked me out of it. Elinor, my eleven year old sister, with Bozo, our Boston terrier, were the family.

As Daddy's voice came over the telephone, my daydreams grew of Los Angeles, Hollywood, Beverly Hills, movie stars. Uncle Eddie was a movie producer. Uncle Morris was a theatrical agent. Uncle Vic and Uncle Reuben both did something in the movies there. *My father would be in the moving picture business!* I had lots of cousins there. One had a radio show. Uncle Eddie was one of the owners of the Palladium Dance Hall, the largest dance hall in the country at that time. Just think what this meant to a girl at my impressionable age. The heavenly cloud continued to grow.

Daddy said, "Sell the house, sell the car and sell some of the furniture. Try to get tickets to come together." Then he stopped. He started to hem and haw. His voice dropped. "Um, uh, well, by the way, you can hardly find an apartment out here so, because of that, you'll just have to sell the dog."

POW!! Away went my dreams..."SELL THE DOG?" I shouted. I dropped the phone.

"SELL THE DOG?" Elinor yelled as she clutched Bozo to her bosom.

"SELL THE DOG?" Mother hollered at me, as if it were all my horrible idea.

"We're not going, Momma. Daddy, we don't care. We're not going."

"Sell the dog?"

The phone swung ominously back and forth by its cord.

By this time, Mother, although upset, was beginning to regret my years of dramatic training.

Daddy, deciding this discussion via telephone over three thousand miles was costing entirely too much money, capitulated and said, "Well, I hope I can find a place to live. I'll try. I love him, too, so don't sell him. We'll do something."

So the rat race began. I get excited and kind of sick to my stomach just remembering. I did think about all the wonderful times we'd had in our sweet little house on 45th Street in Savannah, but I didn't have much time to reminisce. Mother had real estate agents coming through the house to see if they could get us the price we wanted for it. If they didn't think they could, out they went. Sooner than we believed possible, one of them showed up with a man so interested that he would pay for it in cash. That was just wonderful news! Daddy would be so proud of us. I felt so important being in on all the business transactions.

CALIFORNIA, HERE WE COME

I went with Mother to get paid for the house. Our lawyer was there, too. Our purchaser paid us off in crisp green bills. I had never seen so much cash before. Everyone but Bozo and me counted the money. The purchaser counted it first, then the real estate man, the lawyer next, and last, with trembling hands, Momma. She had brought a rather large handbag for the occasion. They all helped her stuff it in carefully. All of us headed out the door, down in the elevator, out to the street, going to the bank across the square to deposit it. My heart was pounding. The lawyer was on one side of mother, the real estate agent on the other.

"Helen, you take Bozo, run to the bank. Look for Mr. Cornell or Mr. Zipperer. Tell them I'm on my way with all this money." I ran all the way, with Bozo on his leash at my heels. (I don't know why we took the dog.) I remember looking back. Mother was the picture of fright, clutching her pocketbook. Each of the men had her by an elbow steering her to the bank and holding her up because her knees were caving in. She finally made it across the square, sighing with relief, plopped the money in front of Mr. Zipperer.

After the money was counted once more and put in the bank, we went to the safety deposit box to collect "important papers." Next we went to the bank president's office He wanted to say how much he loved Momma and Daddy. How he would miss them so. What a lovely man.

We had to get rid of surplus items, also get things packed. Uncle Norman Mirsky brought boxes to the house, tremendous crates that refrigerators came in.

We had to get things packed.

Things came out of closets that I had never seen. Our housekeeper at that time made dozens of trips to the attic. We had all of our current belongings, my sister's wedding presents, and an accumulation of things collected during my parents' married life. Mother took command. She started making groups of things to give away, throw away, or sell. Our *Book of Knowledge* set, Daddy's tackle box. He never went fishing again. He carried on about that for years. Elinor's box of dolls, time for her to grow up.

I definitely was going to give somebody my green tweed coat with the gray fox collar, felt hat, and Girl Scout shoes I wore on my first real date with Herman. Mother said I looked lovely. I didn't believe her then and I don't to this day.

The day came to sell the furniture. It dawned bright and clear. The ad had been in the Sunday issue of the *Savannah Morning News*. Everyone always looked forward to seeing what was for sale, because all kinds of things were hard to get during the war. Mother got tags; we marked all the furniture that was to be for sale. Mother was up bright and cheery.

People came to buy. Mother was in the kitchen selling the stove. I was out on the screen porch trying to sell a young couple the daybed. Elinor and the dog were under everyone's feet. Little did we know what they were up to! When the crowd was at its thickest, we suddenly heard this awful row coming from the living room. We rushed in to find this gentleman and a lady fighting over the best maroon velvet sofa we owned.

He pulled it by the arm toward him.

She yanked it back.

Then he pulled it again.

She yanked it back.

Back and forth it went. It was fascinating!

She started hollering, "I saw it first. I don't care what you say, it's mine, and you just try to get it."

"But"....Mother said.

He gave another tug.

A crowd had gathered to watch the proceedings. Bozo hopped

up on the sofa to get a better view. He cocked his head to one side, as if he knew what was going on.

"I'm sorry, lady. I have my truck in the driveway. As soon as I pay for it, it's mine." He pulled out some bills.

"But ... but..." Mother injected.

Ignoring Mother's buts, they both stood there, glaring at each other.

With a mighty tug, this "lady" heaved it her way one more time, but not until the arm on the sofa cracked right off.

"Oooooohhhhh," the crowd sighed, just like a chorus.

Then silence enveloped the place. Everyone was just stunned. That is, all but my mother who pushed her way through the crowd saying, "BUT — *that* sofa is not for sale."

"Oh," they said.

However, not to be disturbed by the accident and wanting to take advantage of the opportunity, Mother said, "Come in here, look at this chair." The man took "this chair." I think, because he had his truck backed into the driveway, he was too embarrassed to say "no" to whatever Mother suggested. The lady went for the porch daybed, feeling such remorse over breaking the sofa that she kept staying, finally very graciously accepting Mother's invitation to lunch.

Afterward, Mother sat down to count the money. She counted it two or three times. She sat there with a very puzzled expression. "That is funny—I've got more money than I should have." We were both taking in money. We had already counted beforehand how much we would make. Not to have enough money would have been understandable, especially with all the commotion, but too much, hmmmmm? Elinor, the completely mature ten-year-old, looked kind of sheepish.

"While you weren't looking, Bozo and I just went around changing the prices to ten dollars more, because you were just giving the stuff away."

"Elinor, you did?" Mother was shocked.

"Well, come look at that chair in the sun parlor, the man is not picking it up until tomorrow." The chair was the cinnamon and black striped overstuffed velour, which the man was thrilled to have because it was the only thing he'd been able to find large enough to hold his mother-in-law. There on the tag Elinor had erased $25, putting $35 instead. She collected for it, too.

This so won Mother's heart that Elinor was invited to join the "what to sell, give, or throw away group." This was just what Elinor wanted because, by being allowed to be around, she put the very dolls she had been told to give away into a box, telling the men who were packing to take it to the railroad station, with strict instructions to take very good care of them. Their arrival caused quite a stir when they turned up in California. We were to surprise Daddy with many things.

Before we left, if Mother wanted something, she would come in and say, "I've got to write a letter." She got very formal when she meant business. "Have you packed the stationery, too?"

"Yes, in the box marked #3. The northeast corner, half way down under the bank statements is the stationery." I kept a mental file of where I put things. I was eager to go. It's a good thing I remembered where everything was, because many a time Elinor or I hefted ourselves up over the side of the box, going headfirst down in a dive to the bottom to get something. We needed to know where things were. The worst part was that we sold the stove. Eating cold cereal just wasn't keeping up my strength. We couldn't even make a little cup of tea unless we went next door.

Laura, one of our childhood nurses, heard we were going and came to tell us goodbye. She had taken care of me when I was born. She had worked for us off and on for years. I think the last time was when she spent one summer at the beach. She made the most wonderful wild blackberry dumplings.

Laura was pretty old by then, just doing day work. She just wanted to see her babies. She came in and we invited her to sit down. It was a very strange gathering, because she was used to cooking, cleaning, and ordering us all around. That was the last time we ever saw her. We were so glad she came before we left. A cup of tea was brewed next door, and, with a box of stale pretzels, we had a very fine party.

California, Here We Come

We arranged to move in with friends until we could get things finished, so we could go to Asheville to tell my Aunt Charlotte, Uncle Joe, and cousin Gene, goodbye because we'd be leaving them for a long time. In those days transportation was very difficult, because of the war.

As we started out of our house for the last time, Mother suddenly turned as if thunderstruck, running back inside the house She came out with an assortment of brooms, mops, the carpet sweeper, and heaven forbid we should forget, the vacuum cleaner. We piled them all into the trunk of the car. Then back she went again. This time she took a small box, filling it with all the light bulbs out of every socket in the house. I remember feeling quite embarrassed, but for all I knew, it might be a cold dark winter in Beverly Hills.

Now, the reason I have not been telling about Herman is because while all these plans were going on, Herman was out of town. Herman was my first love, destined to be my last. In my heart, I always knew this, but I had to find out how other boys were, to make sure I wanted what I thought I did—him. He never looked at me until I was thirteen and he was fourteen. No matter how much I thought I might like someone else, my Herman was always there. Wherever he went, an imaginary rubber band stretched to bind us to one another. Also my parents wouldn't let me go steady. Oh well, Herman didn't ask me, anyway.

While we were finishing up all the moving details, Herman came home on leave from the Air Force. He looked so handsome in his uniform. We had a wonderful time. He sent me my first orchid. I kept it pressed between the leaves of my mother's dictionary. I still have it.

He gave me his Bar Mitzvah ring. I promised to wear it and I did. He took me out to dinner at the De Soto Hotel night club. Somehow he always made me feel like a queen. His mother asked me if I would wear an engagement ring but I said no, feeling much too young for such seriousness. However, after I went down to the station with his family to tell him goodbye, I wondered if I had made a mistake. Perhaps it would have made him feel we belonged together because then I realized that I might not ever see him again. I went home crying. He went to Italy. I wrote many letters. I also said many prayers for him to be safe.

Time came for us to go to Asheville to visit my aunt, uncle and my cousin Gene. We hoped we could get reservations for California from there. This was to be my longest train ride. We used to go New York on the boat. Once I went to Atlanta on the train, sitting by a very nice young undertaker from Milledgeville in North Georgia, who made me glad I wasn't going to nursing school with a few stories of accidents. How nicely he patched the people up for their funerals. He ruined my taste for lunch, also for the fried chicken he offered me, made for him by his mother.

Mother had gotten a screened cage from Mike who was the *maitre d'* of the ship we used to take to New York before WWII. Into it Bozo was supposed to go. Well, that's what we thought. We opened the door, tried to put his head in the cage. He looked up at us... "Not me," his look at us said. We tried backing him into it. That didn't work either. It finally took Mama, Elinor and me to hold him down, to put his ten pounds of dynamite in that cage. Our hearts ached at treating our precious darling so cruelly. We always pampered him so, or we thought we did until we got to L.A., seeing how dogs were treated there. He turned his little head. He wouldn't look at us. Off with the baggage he went.

All our friends and relatives took us to the station. While we were waiting for the train to leave, we decided to go see how Bozo was making out. We were so worried. Elinor and I went to the baggage cart to see him. He not only didn't speak, but turned his face away from us. We ran around to the other side of the cart, he turned his face away again.

"Bozo, speak to us..."

"Please."

"We're sorry."

"They won't let you on the train any other way. Honest, it's the rules."

"You want to go to California with us, don t you?"

California, Here We Come

We felt how very hopeless our pleas were. He was just crushed. How could we do such a thing to him? Finally, very slowly, he turned his head toward us. I shall never forget as two big tears rolled down his cheeks. Elinor and I burst into tears. We threw our arms around the cage. The three of us cried our hearts out.

We ran to Momma.

"He's ... he's crying."

"He ... he just won't speak to us."

"What'll we do?"

Mother drew up her English-tweed-covered shoulders.

"You, Helen, are eighteen years old. You, Elinor, are eleven. What kind of business is this? Crying? I never heard of such a thing. Dogs don't cry."

"Momma, please go talk to him. Maybe he'll feel better if you go."

In our eyes, Mother was all-healing. She could make anything or anyone feel better.

By this time she was beginning to realize this was serious. After all, she always said Bozo was the only child she had who didn't talk back. She suddenly got quite concerned, making a mad dash for Bozo's cage. She was gone for a few minutes. Then she came back all red-eyed and she said, "You know, he really is crying. I told him not to worry. I told him he'd be all right. We'd see him in a little while but he just cried anyway."

Daddy had told us to sell Bozo!

After we arrived in Asheville, we took Bozo out of his cage. He went back in easily after that, because he then understood its purpose. I guess he thought we were deserting him that first time. He was so much like all of us. You know how people choose dogs to suit their personalities. Well that was it. I have a friend that has a long Grecian nose with honey-colored hair. She has a collie. But we were all small with protruding dark eyes, quick walkers, and excitable personalities. Bozo fit in just fine. He was a Boston terrier.

In Asheville, we waited for Aunt Charlotte and Uncle Joe to come from up the Morganton to pick us up, Mother went to the station's hamburger stand. A crowd had gathered. All of them were munching delectable burgers, as the sign advertised. Mother said to the attendant, "I'd like about fifteen cents' worth of raw hamburger, please."

The man looked at her.

"Raw hamburger?"

"Yes, it's for my dog."

The man looked at Mother as if he wanted to strangle her, so she quickly ordered three more hamburgers for us.

Mother went up to the stationmaster's office to see if he could get us tickets to California. Daddy had a furnished apartment for November 15th. Mother thought she'd use her salesmanship, of which she had plenty, to get us tickets to L.A. So pinning her USO button in her lapel, upstairs she went. After being there a couple of minutes, I looked up to see her looking down, beckoning to us to come up. Knowing how much this meant, we dashed up and put on our most pitiful "we miss our daddy" look, and the stationmaster really felt sorry for Mother and her "little" girls.

Mother was on quite good terms with him for so short a time. I'm sure he thought USO meant United States Officer. We didn't bother to explain. Mother didn't feel guilty; she had a son-in-law in the service. She made many a sandwich for the USO — that's why she had the pin. She had adopted a son to write to in the service. Daddy had done defense work, also served in World War I. He was still getting a pension for the flat feet he got walking all over France. We were entitled to tickets.

We all sat while Mother talked.

The stationmaster listened.

Bozo sniffed around.

It was very quiet. We were tense, very sad looking with our big dark pitiful eyes (Bozo, too).

They talked. Bozo sniffed around.

The stationmaster leaned back, relaxed. He smiled. He made a few more phone calls. He was about to say yes. I could feel it.

I could feel a sign of relief in my throat. It welled up. I put my hand on my chest to take a deep breath. The quiet was overwhelming...

California, Here We Come

At that moment Bo sniffed again at the man's chair, and he very calmly, quietly, and gracefully lifted his leg, sprinkling the rung of the chair—there were carpets, too! We looked at each other. Then we grabbed Bozo. We ran like fury, leaving Mother to rectify things.

We collapsed in Uncle Joe's car, which we found waiting downstairs. We gave Bozo a good chastising. He looked at us as though he didn't understand. Suddenly, he was so innocent.

We stayed in North Carolina for two weeks. Elinor took over my old job watching for shoplifters at the store. I took Miriam's job at the cash register. All in all, it was pretty profitable two weeks for us when we received our salaries, a cardboard suitcase to take along filled with all the things we liked or Uncle Joe had given to us in the store during our stay.

November 12th arrived. We were finally on our way. The stationmaster came down to see us off. We were so grateful to have our tickets for the tourist train on which we were to travel.

The trip to New Orleans was uneventful but as I look back, I think it was because it was a night train. We slept all night. We arrived in New Orleans early with a whole day there. Mother had it all planned. We were to go to the other station for the train we were to take, check our things, feed and walk the dog. Then we would be off to eat our breakfast, afterward having a wonderful day. We rushed to the other station, hurriedly got rid of our things on the train we were taking, made a mad dash to the baggage compartment to look for our precious angel to feed and walk him. We found the cage all right, but our hearts sank to our toes as we realized it was empty.

"Oh, he's gotten out!"

"He's gone."

We groaned.

Mother, as usual, was calm, saying, "Well he couldn't have latched the cage after he got out."

We moaned, "Then someone's stolen him."

About that time a woman who had a rag tied around her head and was sweeping out this enormous empty New Orleans station with one little broom, said, "Listen, sugar, if y'all lookin' for that black dawg, Sam's got 'im."

"Who's Sam?"

"Well," she answered, "he gets the baggage from the other station. He brings it ova hyar. He bees back mos' anytime naow."

Thanking her, we ran out front just in time to see the truck pull up. There sitting in the jump seat like a king, taking in the sights of New Orleans, was Bozo.

Bozo just looked down at us.

The driver said, "Ladies, he jes made sech a fuss an' just begged to git out, so I jes' took him for a little ride."'

Bozo in New Orleans

We thanked him. He had already fed the mutt. Boy, were we angry with Bo. We took him to walk. He decided that every single lamp post in New Orleans needed his approval, plus a few mail boxes and a set of white-wall tires on a convertible.

Finally, he hopped back into his little cage. We were off to the Morning Call Coffee Shop. The three of us were starving for breakfast. We were so worried about Bo, but he didn't have any consideration at all for us.

We had a wonderful day seeing the Cathedral, Antoine's, the Court of the Seven Sisters, the prison of Jean Lafitte. Also a few other houses, I never did understand, but now I think I figured out why they were once famous. We ended our very pleasant day at Arnaud's, looked at the French menus and deciding to leave our food to the discretion of the waiter, who looked very formidable. It turned out to be the specialty of the house, broiled fish. It was Friday.

I can see it all now. The room was dimly lit with old gas fixtures. There was a white tile foyer, as you walked in, with wine-red carpet beyond. The waiters were in their red coats, black pants and bow ties, with napkins over their arms, serving flaming shish kabob on sizzling skewers. Some were scooping Crêpes Suzettes out of a chafing dish, covering them with flaming cherries. The waiters were speaking French to each other. It was more atmosphere than I had ever seen.

As we ate, there was a couple sitting opposite us. They kept looking at us with side glances.

Mother ate.

They looked.

Elinor and I squirmed.

Mother ate.

They finally started staring.

I got so self-conscious, I could hardly eat.

Mother ate.

I gave Elinor a wondering look. She looked back with understanding.

Mother just kept right an eating.

Then the woman pointed at us.

I whispered to Elinor, "Do you think my slip is showing or something?"

At Arnaud's for dinner

She whispered back, "Stand up. I'll see."

Mother finally stopped eating, looking at us with a frown.

"What do you two think you're doing?"

When we explained quietly, she instructed us to go to the ladies' room. Not to act as if we had never been away from home before, Mother was very proper.

Reprimanded, we went to the ladies' room to check my slip, comb our hair, repair my lipstick, and so on. Elinor and I, for a change, were mum. While we quietly did all this, the lady from the table lost no time in putting in an appearance to give us a closer appraisal. Finally, the lady could contain herself no longer.

"Pardon me," she said, "I guess you just couldn't help noticing my husband and I staring at you out there. We were just wondering if you were from abroad or something."

I looked at myself in the mirror. I looked at Elinor. We had all been too excited to bother to look at each other but, suddenly, I saw us as we appeared to others. Mother, in her English tweed suit, British walker shoes, a very smart but man-tailored Knox hat, with a turned down brim and a large pocketbook that looked as if we needed to bring things from the "old country," or else we were headed for a day of shoplifting. I had on a suit with a red jacket, a plaid pleated skirt, socks, brown and white saddle shoes and a scarf on my head. Elinor, the Creole type with her dark hair and tremendous black eyes, was wearing a navy blue jacket with an emblem, a Scottish plaid skirt, brown Girl Scout shoes, and a scarf on her head, too.

What did this woman think? I turned from the mirror and looked at her without answering, my vivid imagination running away with me as usual. I could see her at home telling her friends about these people she'd seen in New Orleans, such a place for intrigue.

Perhaps she thought we were political refugees, escaping Hitler's wrath or Vichy France. Mother looked like the typical English governess. King George had sent Elizabeth and Margaret Rose over here for the duration. Maybe they were secretly touring the country. I could see her telling her friends.

I couldn't decide whether to say, "*Oui, oui,* Madame," sweeping out gracefully. My high school French was really not helping with the menu but was coming in great here.

Then I thought, I should act like *noblesse oblige,* looking down my rather sharp nose to say, "Tut, tut, Madame, cheerio, what, what?" You know, like David Niven, the Englishman.

Then my true nature got the best of me. I wondered if her "or something" just meant "or nothing." I looked into her face with the most phony sincerity I could muster, in my best Savannah, South

California, Here We Come

Georgia, Chatham County drawl, I said, "No Maaaaamam, we're from Savaaaannnnaaah, Gaaaawgia."

Back to the train we went. It was typical wartime travel. Running to the diner to save a place for the three of us proved to be quite exciting.

We made many friends on the train, as we were never at a loss for words. One friend was a Texas soldier. He wore cowboy boots with his uniform and a wonderful white ten-gallon hat. He loved to show us his coin collection, to tell all the tall tales he could about the war or the West. We were fascinated — the first real cowboy we had ever met.

At the crucial point of one story, he reached into the bottom of his duffle bag to show us a coin he had that fitted in with the story he was telling. As he opened his bag, the train gave a jolt, which it was prone to do, and a big pearl-handled gun popped out, sliding across the floor, landing at my feet. I let out a gasp. The only gun I'd ever seen at close range was Daddy's automatic from World War I that didn't have any bullets in it, which was kept way back on the top shelf in the linen closet, in case burglars ever came into the house. (How would we ever get to it, if someone came?)

Well, our uniformed Texan turned to me and said, "It's all right, ma'am. All good Texans carry one."

In Dallas, we had to change engines. As this gave us time to go get Bo, we three traipsed to the baggage car to see him, to feed and walk him. This turned out to be the biggest thrill of our trip through the desert. I was elected to climb up into the baggage car, into this howling mess of dogs to get Bo down for his Dallas inspection. I climbed up with a boost from Mama and Elinor, who eagerly waited. As I got up off my hands and knees after my boost, I was suddenly thrown forward as the engine and baggage car were unhooked. I looked back to see the two of them, horrified, as I was sped away.

Down the track the box car rolled for miles. Grabbing onto boxes, being thrown around, I was petrified that I might put my hand into the crate of some unfriendly monster. When all the animals started to howl, I felt just like joining them. We went about ten miles down the track. I knew I would be hooked to the wrong train, probably end up in Alaska. Finally, they put a new engine on the baggage car. We returned, delivering me, shaking, into the arms of my frightened mother and sister. As the tears rolled down my cheeks, for the first time, we wondered how we got so brave, thinking, *where is Daddy?*

California, Here We Are

I opened my eyes as the man upstairs walked around. For a moment, I couldn't get my bearings. Everything was so strange. I suddenly had a longing for the house in Savannah. All the familiar things I loved: the vine outside my window when I opened my eyes for so many years, that had comforted me with its green leaves and flowers in the spring; the bars on my window that made me feel so safe. I was so confused in this environment.

The man upstairs dropped his shoes on the floor over my head, and I realized I was no longer in Savannah. Living in a furnished place was very strange to me. They even had a collection of china dogs on the coffee table! I had a new appreciation for Mother's lovely things. The family had been over to visit the night before. All Daddy's sisters, brothers, their spouses, plus all the cousins came. Most of them had been to visit in Savannah. I was thrilled at the situation's being reversed, our being in California.

I soon forgot my longing for Savannah. Our family went by the name of "Small." So I became Helen Small. That was an improvement.

The very first California day, Elinor and I got dressed. We were on Reeves Drive in Beverly Hills. We decided to go for a walk. Little did we know where we lived! We stepped out the door of our Spanish-style apartment house, on a lovely tree-trimmed street. Even though it was November, everything was still green. All the apartments were close together, just a couple of stories high, almost on top of each other. We saw many cars passing at the corner. We walked toward the busy street because it looked so interesting and found ourselves on Wilshire Boulevard. Lincoln Continentals went by in droves. We were fascinated.

From Savannah to Hollywood

We took a left turn, walked a block, then suddenly something unbelievable happened! All the stucco buildings were painted white. One was white and gold. It looked like Arabian Nights, the Taj Mahal. As the California sun struck those white buildings, it hurt my eyes. I got so dizzy. I stood on the corner of Wilshire Boulevard and Beverly Drive. Before me were Trabett and Hoffers, Oviatts, the Beverly-Wilshire Hotel, W & J Sloan, Saks Fifth Avenue, the Beverly Hills Brown Derby, Adrian's Dress Salon, Rheingold Jewelers. I gulped! I walked down Beverly Drive as if the street was made of gold. I saw people I thought I knew. As I started to speak, I realized they were movie stars. We looked, mooned, almost swooned, and finally turned our footsteps toward home, where we arrived drunk with reality.

Mother started looking for a house for us to buy. Daddy went to work at my Uncle Eddie's studio. Elinor went to grammar school near our apartment in Beverly Hills. I had to find something to do, so we looked at UCLA. I just could not see how people got from class to class, the campus was so spread out. If they had a bus, I never saw one.

As it turned out, the Army had taken over most of the college for the duration of the war. In addition, it was already November. I had been out of school for a month, so it was too late to start that quarter anyway. A very good excuse!

Mother asked what I wanted to do. Well, nothing really—just breathe. The family didn't like 18-year-olds around the studio. It just wasn't a good idea, especially for one who had hayseed in her ears. One of my aunts suggested a private school in Beverly Hills near us, Woodbury College, a small accredited college. If you went there, you could get a job almost anywhere you wanted in Hollywood. They had a business course that took a year. Maybe by then I could decide more about what I wanted to do. The family thought that Herman and I would be married by then, anyway. It suited me just fine. Every morning I walked up Beverly Drive. As I passed the Beverly-Wilshire Hotel, I stopped to contemplate about Uncle Eddie and Aunt Elsie. They lived at the hotel. Were they up?

CALIFORNIA, HERE WE ARE

As I wondered, a tremendous man (round as he was tall) came out of the hotel walking a chihuahua. It was an amusing sight—this teeny little dog on the leash, led by this huge man! I saw them every morning. Later, I met him, his wife, and the dog at the hotel. The man was a famous director. He and his wife were dear friends of our family. They had an apartment at the hotel, too. They had no children, so the dog was just their life. She had a four-poster bed next to theirs, a little one with a canopy. It matched their bedroom set; it was made up with monogrammed sheets, which room service changed every day. They didn't have to use their ration stamps, as they ate all their meals down in the hotel dining room, so the stamps went to purchase the best meat that could be found for the dog.

I reached school that first day. Straightened my hat, put on my gloves (required), excited to make friends, also to eat my first lunch in Beverly Hills. When it came, I waited for everyone to make for the door but no one moved. Finally, one girl rose from her seat. She just went up, up, up. All six feet of her! She never ended. This long-legged charmer turned to me with this deep "Bankhead" voice, and said,

"Hey, Miss Small, kid, want a Coke for your lunch?"

Not seeing how just a Coke could satisfy us, I asked, "Don't you go out to eat?"

"No place to go except Prince Romanoff's, or the Derby."

In those days, Beverly Hills was not very commercial with fast-food places, as it is now. I was willing to go, I could tell from her tone she thought either I couldn't afford that or else I might as well realize I wasn't Hedy Lamarr. We wouldn't be assets to the Prince. Realizing I didn't have a sandwich, she graciously offered me half of hers. If it had been mine, I would have been glad to give it away, too. Watercress and mayonnaise! I got hep. Every day she brought watercress and I brought mashed avocado.

Sometimes we strolled around Beverly Drive. I loved to go into the store that sold once-worn dresses of actresses, available second-hand at a mere $4,250. I'd visualize each person, where she went in a gold lamé or a fox cape. Sometimes we sat on the steps of the school, eating our sandwiches while Prince Romanoff stood out on his steps bowing to his guests or kissing their hands. He was soooo charming. We saw them all: Clark Gable, Joan Crawford, Ginger Rogers, Pat O'Brien, Van Johnson, Keenan Wynn and many more. Hedy Lamarr was my favorite. She always wandered around Beverly Drive. One day I saw her buying cosmetics in the dime store. I couldn't get over that.

I will say I learned to be the world's worst typist. This was not the fault of the school. I did learn to type to music, though. The rest of the courses I think I passed but I just don't remember. I did not see my tall lunch mate again once we left school until I saw the movie *The Snake Pit*, in which she played an inmate who always walked around with a rose in her teeth. This went on through the entire picture. I couldn't help but think, "Still a vegetarian, eh, kid?"

My life was very busy. I wrote to Herman. I wondered if he would ever get back. No matter whom I met, I would always be an old maid if he didn't return. I dated because we were not engaged. Also there was a lot for me to see, with so many places for me to go. I was always able to see him every night when I closed my eyes while saying my prayers. It was as if G-d had stamped his picture in my brain so I wouldn't forget him while he was away. No chance of that. Why didn't I tell him I loved him?

Every Sunday we all went house-hunting: Mamma, Daddy, Elinor, Bozo, a couple of aunts, cousins and me. Finally, one weekend, we found the house of our dreams, a white stucco house in Beverly Hills. The location was marvelous. I could get the bus to my school, Elinor could walk to her school, also at the next corner there was the Beverly Hills Dog Hospital & Beauty Parlor. To us this was very important. They gave manicures (to dogs) for fifty cents.

One day when I got off the bus as I was returning from school, I heard a siren screaming. All the cars stopped. I froze in my tracks. A white ambulance with a white-uniformed driver raced out of the dog hospital yard. I jumped out of the way to safety. They just missed me by a hair to save some poor French poodle who lived in Beverly Hills.

California, Here We Are

As we walked into our house in Beverly Hills that first day, we were overcome by things we were not used to. The apartment we had been in was so dark. This lovely house had the afternoon sun streaming in. It was Spanish style, not English like Savannah, but we loved it anyway.

The house had loads of rooms, bedrooms, baths, but the solarium won our hearts. It had windows all around with doors opening onto the patio, a garden with a fishpond outside with a bridge across it. There were tremendous green plants against one wall of the solarium. It looked like my idea of heaven after staying with friends and relatives, living in that dark furnished apartment with unfamiliar can openers. Also, I was lonesome for my own bed.

The house was cleaned. We walked in, heading for the solarium to collapse in our favorite chairs we had missed so much. We had never had such a lovely room. Bozo dashed for the sofa. We followed expectantly. However, we were stopped dead in our tracks because where there had been the green houseplants on the wall, there was this horrible ceramic tile fountain. The tiles were black, maroon, blue, and white. A ledge around it was about ten inches high, forming a pool that took up half of the room. It had probably held fish at one time. On either side of the fountain was a seat. Against the wall was a ceramic tile area with a small basin and a ceramic head that spit water into the basin, which overflowed into the large pool. How did we miss that thing?

We were astounded. Mother and Daddy couldn't sleep that night. It was forever referred to by Daddy as "that damned thing." We stumbled over it, cursing it. Even Mother, who never even said "damn," was in accordance with us. Finally, on one of their sleepless nights they spent worrying, Mother had an idea.

"How about building round steps that would fit over it. I'll cover it with plants."

Daddy thought that would be a good idea. Not being one to procrastinate, Daddy had men from the studio come out the next day to build steps from his design. Believe me, this took detailed plans. We covered it with lovely green plants in beautiful pots. It looked pretty for a long time but, since no one in our family can miss hearing anything, the plants were pushed aside so we could sit there. We all got too busy to water all fifty-nine plants, so something had to be done. The plants started to droop.

One day Daddy was home sick in bed. Mother took Bozo to go shopping. When Mother came back, some men from the studio were there. Daddy was directing from the sofa. Chisels, hammers, and dust were going every which way. Out went the fountain. We were very happy afterward, because we replaced it with chairs. That fountain had a personality that lived on, though. It had given us much consternation, but also many laughs.

One day a lovely lady rang our door bell. She told Mother she had once lived in our house; she had loved it so much and wondered if we had enjoyed it as much as she did. Mother invited her in but she declined, saying she just wanted to know who was living there now. They chatted a little, and then came the real purpose of her visit. As she was getting ready to leave, she drew herself up proudly, saying in this loving tone, "You know, I just can't leave without telling you that we are the people who put the fountain in."

As she made this glowing remark, I could see Mother's back stiffen. Oh, brother, did this lady put her foot in it. Mother, never failing to rise to the occasion, but not to be outdone, threw back her shoulders very proudly and answered, "Well, you know what? We are the people who took it out."

It took us a while to get unpacked. We had unpacked all the necessary items. Every now and then we'd unpack a box that Mother had brought that didn't contain vital things — a box there was no rush to get to.

When we got to the kitchen things, Daddy really blew his stack. Empty jars, a jar of dried beans! He said, "The beans sat on the shelf in Savannah for a year. Do you think you'll use them, Sweetheart? They also have empty jars here, too, you know."

Mama looked at him with such tolerance answering, "Well, Sweetheart, it didn't cost any more to bring them." They just kept "sweethearting" back and forth. That's what they always called each other.

Herman wrote to me from Italy. We were both living fantastic lives. My life was more fun than his was. He wasn't having fun at all.

Our family lived near Carthay Circle. The movie theater there was just as famous as Grauman's Chinese for lavish premieres. Inside, it had lush carpets you just sank into, with beautiful paintings of the early West on the walls. My sister and I used to go over to watch people going to the premieres. Lights, cars, sirens, cameras were flashing. Then later I would go to the dress shop on Beverly Drive to see some of the dresses worn at the premiere. Daddy used to bring us things from the wardrobe department for us to wear. My greatest treasure was Shirley Temple's raincoat, which I wore, loving it dearly. I had some of Ann Bancroft's things that Daddy sent to me after I was married and moved to Savannah.

At the Office and Other Things

Aunt Elsie and Uncle Eddie invited me to come to the Beverly Wilshire pool on the weekends. I took one of my girlfriends, who wanted to be an actress. We had quite a group. I was always looked upon as the naïve one. My friends were the sexy Hollywood types. We got to know each other because our mothers were friends. A lot of my time was spent with Harry Ritz, the comedian, and Carlos Romeras, the Colombian opera star. Harry Ritz was just as funny without a script as he was with one. He always told dirty jokes until I came around. However, my job was to keep score when he and Carlos played gin rummy for $100 a point. I bring this up because it was standard procedure there, but some of the people I know would be stunned, even if they could afford to do it themselves. It was a lot of money in those days.

I left school because my uncles offered me a job in the theatrical agency. What more could one ask for? As I picked up things quite easily, I was confident I could do the job. So, thrilled to the teeth, off I went to The Small Agency. This is where all the girls in the family would get a taste of being out in the world. They were still watched over by Uncle Reuben and Uncle Morris. I must say they did a good job.

I was ushered into my own office. The building was on Sunset Boulevard, right in the heart of the most interesting part of Hollywood. All within walking distance were the great Garden of Allah, the most famous of all Hollywood hotels, many magnificent mansions, and famous night clubs: the Mocambo, Ciro's, Bit of Sweden, and The Players. There was also Schwab's Drugstore, the most famous drug store in history.

The Small Company building, having been a night club previously, had a large center lounge with chairs, couches, lamps, and so on. You walked into a tremendous carpeted room, the sofas had satin upholstery with grey wood arms. In the center of the room was a table, where beautiful flowers were kept. My favorites were the Birds of Paradise. All the other offices were off this center room. The switchboard operator was in a glass cage in the lobby. The extra offices were rented to a producer, an author, and a singers' agency.

Upstairs was another group. I never bothered to find out what they did, but one day they did bring in this young fellow who had written "The Ballad for Americans." I was introduced. We had a nice little chat. I shall never forget him because I think that is one of the most wonderful pieces of Americana there is.

My first few days as a stenographer caused me to carry many a letter home in my pocketbook, to tear up, after I had typed the corrected ones; I was afraid to throw them in the trash. I learned that this is a very common practice among new stenographers. I burned them in the incinerator at home.

In addition to taking dictation and doing letters, I answered Jack Oakie fan mail. I had an electric typewriter, the wonders of science. Timid as I was, that thing was not much help. I fought with this modern piece of equipment, but succumbed to its charm because I soon learned how wonderful it was. Fortunately, as my predecessor had known she was leaving, she let the fan mail pile up. There were thousands of letters. Mr. Oakie got tremendous fan mail from Hawaii and England, where they loved him.

I also learned to operate the switchboard. Going in early, I'd run back and forth between my desk and the switchboard until the operator came in. If the board was busy, I just stayed in the cage stuffing Jack Oakie pictures into envelopes, then stamping them for mailing.

One day I was in this tremendous office all alone. (I look back at this in amazement. They left me in charge.) Everyone disappeared at lunchtime. This producer came in. I'd never met him, but I had been warned about him. I was sitting in my office. He came in and perched on my desk, a true Hollywood "wolf." I got a little nervous. If he was making a movie, he'd have a list of starlets.

He dated them before starting the picture. The ones he liked, he hired for the movie. The ones he didn't, well—rather an odd way to pick talent? Such is life. Not all producers were like that; in fact, very few.

He offered me a cigarette. I declined, saying I didn't smoke. He kidded me about it, then told me his name. I was new, he didn't know me. I didn't tell him my name.

"Well, can I buy you a drink?" he asked.

"No, sir," I replied.

"Well, you little ole Southern belle, if you don't drink and you don't smoke, what is your vice? You must have one."

"Yes sir, bein' from the South, I chew a little tobacco."

I hoped he would find this humorous, also a little nauseating, and leave me alone, but he was more interested than ever. At that moment, Uncle Morris came in. Seeing the situation, he introduced me very plainly as his niece. Guess what? After that, all I could get from that producer in the way of conversation was a request for phone call messages with a curt "hello." That was just fine with me.

Uncle Morris Small

I loved my job; the office had in the past handled many of the greatest in the entertainment business. There were many famous people discovered and represented by my uncles.

Uncle Morris ran the agency. He was loved by everyone and by me. He still lives in my wonderful memories of him. I used to take dictation in his office. I typed all my letters, plus daily reports of his visits to the studios for the actors' files.

Our office handled Jack Oakie, Lionel Barrymore, Percy Kilbride, Ethel Barrymore, Leonid Kinsky,

At the Office and Other Things

William Demarest, Dane Clark, Douglass Dumbrille, Norma Varden, Gladys Cooper, Eva Gabor, Zsa Zsa Gabor, Sir Thomas Beechman and many others. In the past they had handled Jean Harlow, Norma Shearer, John Payne, Valentino, Lupe Velez, Anthony Dexter, plus many more. I used to go down into the basement and read their files. What a look into the past.

Jack Oakie was one of my favorites. He did so love to tease. He adored his wife, Venita. There was never anyone else for him, but they were always having their ups and downs. The part I loved was that whenever they broke up, her mother always went with Jack to take care of him. We used to keep his personal books.

Finally, he and his wife were supposedly breaking up for good. He was to give her a settlement in one lump sum. He would have agreed to anything because he loved her so. I had to type out the check for that. When Uncle Reuben, who was the accountant, brought it to me, I nearly fainted. It took me three checks to get it correct. I had never written a check for $103,000 before or since. I kept shaking, making mistakes. I couldn't get it all in that little space. Finally, I got it. I never did get to see it cancelled, but I'm sure it came back. I used to love to look through Jack's files. He had once been so magnificently handsome.

A few years later, he was to be reunited with his wife again. They were to fly to New York to be remarried. Uncle Morris was to take Jack to the plane, but Jack was too ill to go at the last minute. Venita went on without him. As fate would have it, the plane crashed. All were killed. After that, Jack Oakie faded from public view. I almost believe he wished he could have been on that plane, too.

Another favorite was Lionel Barrymore, who was so very wonderful. The Small Agency handled the whole family: John, Ethel, and Diana when I was there. John was already dead. Ethel and Diana were in New York, so the only one I knew was Lionel. He was then on *Mayor of the Town*. He was also in the Doctor Kildare series, working from a wheel chair. Although very crippled by arthritis, he still painted, wrote music, acted, and drove his own car. He used to come by once a week to pick up his check. I would take it out to his car. He always came when everyone except me was out to lunch and I was on the switchboard. He would make me prop the door open so I could hear the board ring. It was always quiet at lunch time so it was all right. We'd discuss that week's *Mayor of the Town* broadcast or his latest picture, the most recent concert of his music at the Hollywood Bowl — what a genius he was. He acted as if he valued my opinion so much. If I liked something, he'd be so thrilled.

He and Uncle Morris were friends. When Uncle Morris passed away, Mr. Barrymore came to the funeral to give the eulogy. He said in part, "Whenever anything went wrong, Morris would put his hand on my shoulder, saying, 'Don't worry, son, everything will be all right.'" Barrymore was much older than Uncle Morris. He said he expected Uncle Morris to greet him at those Pearly Gates and to tell him that he knew everything would be all right, just like he said.

Percy Kilbride was one of my dearest friends. If you're old enough, you will remember him as "Pa Kettle." He dressed just like the timid little Englishman he was. He wore a derby hat, with a black suit. He always carried an umbrella even if it wasn't the rainy season. He brought us flowers from the florist across the street, never missed a time. He talked in a very low nasal tone, almost a whisper so that you had to listen very carefully to hear him. He was so shy, and very nervous, I don't know how he ever became an actor. He had terrible mike fright. He had wonderful offers to go on radio but was always too scared to accept them.

How sad it is to see people who are wonderful great talents with nothing to do. Leonid Kinskey was the most "Roosian" Russian I have ever met. He played roles similar to Mischa Auer. Kinskey was in *Les Miserables, The Great Waltz, Story of Irene and Vernon Castle, I Married an Angel,* and so many others. However, he was so definitely a type that after a while there were not many parts for him. His accent was impossible. No matter what he said to me, I always answered, "yes." That was the right thing to do because his face used to light up. He talked on at great length with such life and enthusiasm.

AT THE OFFICE AND OTHER THINGS

Leonid loved perfume. He always wanted to know what kind we wore. If he brought you some perfume, it usually was one he thought suited your personality. He brought me some called "Little Flower." Later he had parts on television. I saw this man playing bellhops or elevator boys. It hurt me so. That is why it is better not to get show business in your blood because its disappointments seem to hurt even more than other ways of life.

One day Bill Demarest came in like a winter storm. He always played the big tough Marine sergeant and the grandfather on *My Three Sons*. He was just like that, too. He was nice, but with lots of noise, laughter, and jokes. He loved guns. This particular day he came in with his latest prize, a silver-handled pistol. It was a magnificent thing. Believe me I had a real opportunity to find out.

He asked me to take a letter from him. As I sat down with my book, he asked if I liked the gun. Then as he pointed it at me, I nodded vigorously to the affirmative. I was too shaken to answer aloud. Seeing how frightened I was, he thought that was a great joke. Leveling it at my head, he said, "Okay, kid, write." Believe me I wrote. He never moved the gun the whole time he dictated the letter to me.

Eva Gabor was also handled by our office. I had never seen anyone so gorgeous in person. In those days, she was just starting out. Whenever she had an appointment at the studios, she wore a black suit trimmed with white mink with little mink tails on the collar and on the white mink muff she carried. Her whole outfit was very beautiful.

There were many other lovely character people. Gladys Cooper and Norma Varden were two of my favorites. They played aunts or mother roles. Arlene Dahl was a starlet then. I always knew that someday she would be famous. Douglass Dumbrill always plays an English hunter in a pith helmet. He was a very handsome man. He married Alan Mowbray's daughter, half his age. I don't blame her. I'd have married him if he'd asked me.

Herbert Rudley played a businessman. Rudley had a different hairpiece for different parts. If it was for an older man, he had a thin hairpiece streaked with gray but for a younger man, a thicker one. He would bring them to the office to try them on for us to decide which one looked best for the part he was trying to get.

Some people had long-term contracts. Those people usually never came into the office. They were "set." There were the people who worked for so much a picture. Next were people who received a guarantee of so many weeks' work at so much per week. Next came the people who were guaranteed one week's work. Last were the ones who worked by the day. They were glad to work two days a month at $150 per day. I used to feel so sorry when I would write out those checks. Then Friday came when I wrote my own check for a whole week. I never felt sorry for anyone else again.

Perhaps you've never heard of David Street. He had a career as a singer and was on the way up. He trained the boys' choir that sang in *Going My Way*. He was adorable, handsome, and friendly. I loved him to come into the office, he acted so young and innocent. His agent gave a case of assorted whiskey to him, with a lengthy discussion on how to mix drinks. He knew nothing when it came to mixing drinks, that's how ignorant he was. One day when he came into the office at lunchtime, he found me there alone. I thought nothing of it when he said he'd wait for his agent, Sam. He asked me if I was alone. Typing a daily report, I didn't even look up when I answered, "Yes." Then he called me out into the lobby. I wandered out of my office completely off guard.

"Well," he said, "Sugar, I hope you can run fast today. You had better get started. If I catch you, I'll kiss you like you've never been kissed."

I didn't wait to see if he was joking. I had begun to learn about Hollywood, and by this time I had already bolted up in the stairs, running through all the connecting offices, slamming doors behind me as I went. He came laughingly after me. As I flew back down the steps, looking back to see if he was catching up, I fell, twisting one of my ankles. I stumbled, just making it to one of the sofas in the lobby. He grabbed me, throwing his arms around me, and kissed me for all he was worth. I was thrilled. He later married and divorced Lois Andrews (George Jessell's ex-child bride). I don't know what ever happened to him, but I read he had four or five wives. My, how he changed from the shy lad I first knew.

However, all was not gaiety. There was a singers' agent in our office. I don't remember his name, but he had become quite famous. He went back to visit his native town as the Big Hollywood Agent. While there, he met this shy, sweet girl. She was not thin or glamorous but, then, neither was he. She did have the most beautiful face you have ever seen. He was so thrilled by her shy, sweet manner and sensitive face that he asked her to marry him the first day they met. She married him, returning to California as his charming bride. She had two children right away. Unfortunately, she was not the type to adjust easily. Being shy, she was very lonesome, really lost in Hollywood among her husband with his friends. He worked all day, taking out his clients at night so that they could be seen, perhaps hired. She never went. It was not her kind of life.

Finally, in desperation, she came to work in his office so she could at least see him, to be with him during the day. This is where I met her. We became very close. We used to talk a lot, especially when all the men and the other secretaries went out to lunch, and we were there alone. When I left to get married, she told me she was expecting their third child. She didn't know how to tell her husband. It made me feel sad, that she had such a problem. I left, that was the last time I saw her.

After I married, I went back to L.A. for a visit. I ran into my agent friend at a restaurant on the Strip. I spoke. We had a big reunion. I didn't ask about his wife; I was terribly embarrassed, because we had been such dear friends, but I couldn't remember her name. How could I forget? My radar equipment was constantly at work. I noticed he acted rather strangely. I thought surely his feelings were hurt because I had neglected to ask about his family.

As my cousin and I walked to our table, I mentioned the agent's wife to her. "Well, thank heaven you didn't ask about her. He was probably afraid you would." Then she told me this story: They did very well and he bought a large estate. She didn't want such a big, lavish place, but he had to have it. He entertained at home on a large scale, and he also still went out every night with his people. All she wanted was her husband, her children, and a small quiet place where they could be happy. Their worlds were too far apart. One night when he was out, she turned on the gas and stuck her head in the oven. She killed herself, but he got there before the gas fumes asphyxiated the children. I guess she felt he'd be better off without her and she was ashamed to go home.

I never met Lupe Velez, the Mexican spitfire, but I feel I knew her well. The bus I took to go to work went all through Beverly Hills. On the bus were two other girls who worked at the Zeppo Marx Agency. One of the girls left to get married in Las Vegas with a hairpin as a wedding band. The other girl, Toni, had once been a WAMPAS Baby Star, and she was still very cute. She had been dating the agency's client, a French man, who gave her up for Miss Velez.

The bus we rode every day took us right smack past Lupe Velez's house. The Frenchman's car was usually parked in her driveway when we rode by. If it was not there, we'd dash to the office, grab the *Hollywood Reporter* or *Variety* to read the gossip column. Sure enough, there would be an article about how Lupe and her boyfriend had had an argument. Nothing was a secret. Then Toni and I would call each other to discuss it.

One day I rode up on the bus alone as Toni was off from work. I always passed the Velez house at 8:45 on the dot. That day I looked for her beau's car. It was not there. I ran into the office. There wasn't a thing in the papers about a fight between the two of them. I couldn't wait until the next day to discuss it with my friend. I plugged in the switchboard. I thought about calling her at home but then felt silly. I licked stamps, putting them on the fan mail envelopes. (It was a tough job, but somebody had to do it.) I waited for everyone else to come in at 10:00.

About 9:45, the door to the office exploded open. Men with flash cameras came fighting, flying through the door, screaming, "Where is Mr. Small?"

"He's not here. No one gets here until later."

"Well, sister, we just came from Lupe Velez's house. She killed herself. This office used to handle her. We want all the pictures and information you have on her."

I looked at them as if I didn't understand what they were saying. No, no, it just couldn't be. This was out of my category. I thought I was going to throw up. They were in a big hurry. I told them I would find what I could. I went downstairs to the basement, which had once been a wine cellar. It was now used for dead files (no pun intended). I got out whatever files we had on Miss Velez. Afterwards, shaking, I had to pull myself up the steps by the rail.

When I got upstairs, the reporters showed me copies of the death note. Then these men went in different offices calling their papers, reporting their story. The switchboard was buzzing like crazy. I was so stunned that the only thing I remember about the death note was that she asked that someone please take care of her dogs. I knew she was pregnant. Everyone knew she wanted her beau to marry her, but he wouldn't. Most people thought she just tried to scare him. Seems she had tried to kill herself many times before.

I gave the reporters her file. Uncle Morris came in. He gave them whatever information he could.

Venita Oakie called the office to say that she had been the last to see her. They lived near each other. As Venita walked her own dogs at about 3:00 a.m., Lupe called down to her from her bedroom window. They talked for a few minutes. The L.A. papers carried full page spreads of the story for days. Just think, as I rode by her house that day, she was upstairs in her room dead. They found her a few minutes after nine that morning.

When I first went to work, one of the secretaries took me under her wing. We went to lunch, she introduced me around Schwab's Drugstore. It wasn't until Uncle Morris fired her that I found out that she was not the type of girl my family wanted me to pal around with. She was so nice, too. I loved to go to lunch with her because she just knew everyone. I couldn't tell by looking at her that she was a high-priced call girl.

One day she introduced me to a man called George, who did some acting. He was older, grayhaired, very sophisticated. He told me about his daughter, who was my age. He had the loveliest manners. We enjoyed many a lunch together, sitting at the lunch counter at Schwab's.

One day Daddy sent the studio limousine for me. Who should be working on the set in a bit role but George? He saw me with Daddy and Uncle Eddie. He was very friendly. Daddy asked how I knew him, so I told him. I was warned to have nothing to do with

him. Then the story came out that he had stolen some of a Mrs. Spreckel's jewels, many thousands of dollars' worth. She was the young trophy bride of a multimillionaire, and she gave parties when he was out of town. George was caught, but they made a deal; she wouldn't prosecute if he wouldn't tell about her wild parties. So he told the paper he took her jewels to scare her and play a joke because she always left her things lying around. He gave the jewels back. After that I stayed out of his way.

One day as I came out of the bank, next to Schwab's, George called to me from his convertible. I waved. He was with a friend. The friend stepped in front of me. George introduced us, asking if I wanted to go to the horse races with them. I thanked him, refusing, then turned around to leave. As I did, the other man blocked my way.

George told him, "Pick her up."

With that, this big clunk picked me up, lifted me over the side of the car, depositing me on the seat, and he jumped in beside me so I couldn't get out.

"Now, Baby, we're going to the races." I pleaded to get out. George started the motor to get out of his parking place.

He said, "I bet your family would pay plenty to get you back."

I started to think about the stories I'd heard about him. Toni had told me he beat up one of her girlfriends on a date.

I started talking fast, "They don't want me. They wouldn't care if I died. They wouldn't pay a wooden nickel for me. If you don't let me out, I'll scream so loud you'll go back to jail for sure, forever."

I opened my mouth to scream. He clapped his hand over my mouth. He must have believed me because he changed his mind.

"Let her out," he told his friend.

A few months later, Daddy came home with the newspaper, holding it up so I could see the front page and headlines. There on the front page was George's picture with two-inch headlines stating that he was the head of the largest counterfeit ration stamp gang on the West Coast. Needless to say, he went to jail. My "kidnapping" was always considered a great joke until he went to jail. Since then it just doesn't seem so funny anymore.

There were times on the weekend when they worked on a movie, and Daddy would send the studio limousine for me. The chauffeur would usher me into this 20-cylinder, leather-upholstered, shiny vehicle. I gracefully climbed in—no great star could have done better. Once inside was a different story. It was a fight for life! He took off at 45 mph, he went around the corners on two wheels. I was all alone in the back. First, I'd cling to one strap, then, as we went around a curve, I would slide across those leather seats as if my bottom had been greased, then wham. Up against the other side I'd go with a thud.

I was separated from the front by a glass window. The limo didn't have a phone in the back, so I couldn't call him. Anyway, I was too busy holding on. We finally would have to slow down for the guard at the studio gate. I'd smooth my hair, cross my legs, acting just as though I was Hedy Lamarr. I smiled at the guard as he greeted me, waving us through. Then off we'd go again, going around the corner, skidding to a stop in front of the sound stage where Daddy was waiting. I always thanked the driver, but I really wanted to bop him one.

One day on the set of *Abroad with Two Yanks*, I was having a wonderful time visiting with all the actors and actresses. Dennis

O'Keefe, William Bendix, John Loder, Marilyn Maxwell, plus Rochester, were in the picture. Rochester (who played Jack Benny's chauffeur on radio and television) loved Daddy's Southern accent. He followed Daddy around just to hear him talk. Bendix and O'Keefe were dressed up like women that day. Dennis O'Keefe had on a blue satin dress, an ostrich fan, with a blonde wig. Looking up at his six feet of loveliness, I said, "Mademoiselle, you must be the pin-up girl of the whole Army."

"No," he said, "but I'm the throw-up girl of the Navy."

They worked all day on one scene; finally, everyone remembered their lines. All costumes were correct. They all breathed a sigh of relief as the director said to call it a take. They had done the same thing so many times, they were exhausted. I was too, from just watching. It was over. Everyone was happy but that was short-lived. Uncle Eddie walked up from the back of the set where he had been quietly sitting, saying,

"It was terrible. Re-write it, and then shoot the whole thing again tomorrow."

Everyone just groaned.

We had lunch that same day at the commissary. It was Shirley Temple's birthday, and she was there. They brought a cake. We all sang "Happy Birthday," having a piece of cake. That day Orson Welles and Joseph Cotton sat across from us. I stared fascinated at Orson Welles. Those black eyes stared back at me over a chocolate soda he was having. We both laughed as Mr. Cotton lifted Mr. Welles up to leave.

Later on, after the picture was finished, we went to see a sneak preview of it in Burbank. I don't know why, but I was a nervous wreck, always feeling that way when I went to see my uncle's pictures. This time Daddy was responsible for it, too. After the picture was over, people wrote their opinions on cards. We waited with Uncle Eddie, Dennis O'Keefe, and William Bendix. It was exciting to be part of such a moment. The cards were very favorable. They liked the ending, too, so there would be no re-takes on that! It turned out to be a hit. "King Midas," as Uncle Eddie was called, did it again.

Going to Glamorous Hollywood Places

I kept busy, trying not to worry about Herman, writing to him every day, but still wanting to see everything there was to see in California, too, which I did. I went to all the different places I could. I remember dinner at Ciro's cost ten dollars! Wow, what a lot of money in 1943. I loved the Mocambo best of all, though.

The Beverly Hills Tropics was like walking into another world once you went through the door. Earl Carroll's show was the most extravagant stage show I have ever seen in my whole life. These magnificent creatures came down steps in lavish costumes. I guess it was the West Coast Follies. I returned years later. It was no longer the gorgeous, breathtaking place it once was. The program *Queen for a Day* was held there. It is not there anymore, either.

Across the street from Earl Carroll's was the Palladium. They were very strict about serving drinks to minors. They kept it a clean, nice place, with a milk bar upstairs for the young people. I saw many famous bands there, but the most magical moments I spent there were when I heard Artie Shaw play the drums. I am definitely not the "love to listen to the drums type," but he was the greatest, most unbelievable drummer I have ever heard. Everyone waited, holding their breath, until he came on. The lights went on over his drums. He walked in to the roar of clapping, it was deafening. He did not disappoint us.

Daddy got us tickets to some of the radio shows, too. One day Elinor and I were the guests of Garry Moore. He was supposed to make a movie at the studio, but he couldn't act. He was funny in his show on television, but it didn't work out for the part they wanted him to play in the movie.

From Savannah to Hollywood

Frank Sinatra was the person who had the most magnetic personality. I swooned with all the rest of the girls. If he were still alive, I would still swoon over him with all the rest of the mamas and grandmamas. He was this ugly, tiny guy with bad skin, but in those days he could really sing. Kids screamed, hollered, jumped up and down. The studio used to get me tickets to his radio show.

One of the dear friends I met was a young man called Harvey, who had been doing quite well at MGM before the war as a writer. He volunteered for the Navy and his ship was torpedoed. He was adrift in a life raft with two other fellows for eighteen days. He had malaria, as well. When they were rescued, one of the fellows was dead, the other two were not even conscious.

When Harvey was sick, not being able to see me, he wrote beautiful poetry, mailing it to me. One time we had a date lined up. He got a malaria attack at the last moment, sending a friend of his instead. His friend dated me a couple of times. The entire time, the man talked about Lauren Bacall or Betty, as he called her. He had dated her many times in New York before she became famous. I thought, "I'm about as far as you can get from that type. You won't want to date me." I was right. He never called me after two dates.

Some of my dates were boys from Savannah, passing through California to the Pacific. I took them to The Bar of Music, which had twin pianos. Ravel's "Bolero" or the "Ritual Fire Dance" on twin pianos was incredible.

I went to the Hollywood Canteen a couple of times but it wasn't worth the trouble. You just were squashed in the crowd.

Another man I spent time with was a photographer, Frank, who asked my parents if I could go out with him because he was an older guy. He was not eligible to go into the service because of his health and age. He loved to take pictures of me, not in the nude or anything. He had studios set up in different stores in L.A. He took pictures of me, enlarging them, printing them, in sepia, black and white, or he would tint them (no colored film in those days) so that clients could get an idea how the different photos looked. Sometimes I would pass a storefront seeing a whole window of

Going to Glamorous Hollywood Places

myself staring back at me. It was quite a shock. I never took any pictures of them. That was stupid!

Frank took me to dinner at all the famous places. We'd go to dance or to a show of some kind. Afterward, we would end up at Barney's Beanery. Now, this was a very famous place. It was about the size of a small living room or a large postage stamp. In the middle was the cook stove. A stand-up-to-eat bar ran around the stove, three booths were to the side of that. If there were people at the bar, you played the devil getting past them to the booths.

On the stove was a big black pot, stirred by a Gravel Gertie look-alike from Dick Tracy. It had to be her! She was skinny, her dress hung on her long twig arms, her white hair fell down her back. She stirred the chili with a big, long spoon. My mouth still waters at the thought of that chili, as the very best came out of that pot.

Even though I enjoyed myself, going to all the wonderful places in Los Angeles with different fellows and friends I had met, I wrote Herman every day. I got mail from him, too. Mine was an existence in two lives; one, writing to Herman, worrying about him, and the other, seeing things in Los Angeles. These were opportunities I would never have again.

Heavy Hearts

As time passed, I was more concerned about whether Herman and I would ever see each other again, or get together when he came back. I still kept the letters going.

One week I didn't hear from Herman. I used to call Momma every day to see if a letter had come from him. One week stretched into two. I knew that soldiers were moved to different theaters of war but somehow, in my heart, I just knew something had happened to him. I was not a pessimist, but the rubber band that stretched half way around the world from him to me told me so. One day I got the courage to tell Mamma that I didn't feel that Herman was dead, but somewhere he was in trouble.

Mother started to choke up. "Your father told me the same thing last night."

Hearts were heavy in our house. Of all the boys I had ever gone with, Herman was the one we all loved dearly. Momma and Daddy were so very worried, too. I kept calling home every day at lunchtime to see if I had gotten a letter. On one particular day, Mother sounded so very gay on the phone that I wondered what had gotten into her, since I knew how concerned she was. I guess I should have known that she was just putting on a face for me. She had Aunt Elsie over there when I called and kept her there all day so that when I came home that night, she would have courage to tell me the truth.

When I arrived home from work that day, Mamma took me by the arm, walking me back to her bedroom. Now that I am a mother myself, I just don't know how she ever had the strength to live through that moment. She sat me down on her bed.

"Helen," she started. Then I knew. Oh, how I knew. She didn't have to say another word. Momma showed me the newspaper clippings our friends had sent. Herman was missing in action. People just didn't make phone calls in those days, the way they do today.

My first reaction was, "It's all my fault." I started to cry.

"I didn't have faith that he would be all right. If I'd had, this wouldn't have happened." At that moment, I regretted all the frivolous things I had been enjoying. I wanted to do whatever I could to punish myself for not marrying him; for not making him happy before he went away. Little did I realize how even more tragic it would have been, if we were married, spending only a short time together. I felt that I had had my chance to make his life happy. I didn't do it. I also felt the terrible loss of not experiencing those few precious moments of love from him.

Mother finally calmed me down. Herman was missing over Hungary. No official word had come from the War Department as yet, but Herman had an uncle, Arthur, who was only six years older than Herman. He was also in the Air Force. They were both in the Italian theater of war, and they had been trying to see each other. Finally, Arthur got some days off, going to Herman's base, only to be told Herman had been shot down three days before.

According to Arthur's letter home, German fighters came right into Herman's squadron's formation, firing machine guns and cannons as their plane entered the bomb run over Budapest. Seven members of his crew were seen to have parachuted down before the plane exploded in mid-air. The bomb load was not dropped. Their parachute jump was a delayed one, Arthur wrote, meaning that the men got below the flak, and the bombers flying behind them, before pulling their ripcords. The fact that seven were seen to pull their cords indicated they were conscious, having an excellent chance of surviving and of being prisoners of war in Hungary.

In my heart I just couldn't accept the fact that he might be dead! I took out the last letter he had written to me. He mailed it July 11, 1944. He was shot down July 14, 1944. He wrote this to me:

Dear Helen,

I really haven't much to say at this time, but since I've been thinking about you all day today, I thought maybe

I'd write. My thoughts went back a hundred years, or so it seemed anyhow. Did you ever think back about the good times we used to have together? Remember when I was about 14 and you about 13, I took you out for the first time to the tea dance they had at Junior High School and, boy, it really was something when I found out that I couldn't dance. I was never so embarrassed in all my life. No kidding, and then out at Isle of Hope, the first time we kissed, remember that? If it weren't for you, I don't think I'd ever have gotten up the nerve. Sure was a timid kid in those days, eh? Every time I look back on those days it tickles hell out of me. Then during those later days, I guess I was just as bad but at the time you couldn't have convinced me of it. Sometimes I even thought I was quite the "coxman." Maybe I'm just as bad now but as usual I don't think so because after all I have been around a little this past year....

My heart broke. I was so impressed with his very important thoughts.

He was twenty, a lieutenant, a bombardier. He really had been around.

I wrote to his parents and they kept me informed about any new happenings. They contacted and wrote to the families of all the men on the plane. They were informed by the War Department that he was missing. They would be informed as soon as his whereabouts were learned, if he was a prisoner. It was four months before we heard he was in German hands.

After we learned at what prison camp he had been placed, I started to write every day on special "prisoner of war" paper that I got from the Post Office. As long as I kept writing though, he seemed to remain close. Somehow my faith grew, becoming a conviction that he would come back. I finally got two cards written from him in prison camp. He told me to keep my chin up. That he would see me soon. After seeing the pictures of the prisoners in magazines, it was not easy, but I made up my mind that I would do so for him.

Going to the Academy Theater

I worked, trying to keep busy. I now spent more time with my family. We went every week to the Academy of Arts and Sciences Theater in Beverly Hills. You have to be a member to attend. The members are the people who, every year, vote on the Academy Awards. They have two features twice a week. Mother and Daddy had this group of friends who'd meet there, usually Uncle Vic came, the Whytocks, the Andersons, and us. They would save seats in a certain section of the loges. If it was time for the movie to begin, if not all were present or accounted for, the others would have a big discussion as to what had happened to the missing one.

"Did you talk to him?"

"Is he ill?"

"Are you sure he's all right?"

Howard Anderson had a movie studio that made miniatures, you know, like miniature volcanoes, wars, and such. If something had to be blown up, his studio made things to scale: oceans, battleships, mountains, continents, and so on, then they put a little firecracker to them and boom! When you saw it, Nagasaki! They do all that with computers now.

One night it was my birthday. After the show, Mr. Anderson invited me to come over to his car as he had a birthday present for me. He opened the door of the car, the light went on. I just gasped. You see, he grew orchids as a hobby. On the back seat of his car was an orchid plant in full bloom. It had been grown from seed, taking eight years to bloom. This huge plant with twenty-five blossoms on it was a sight to behold. I asked him to let me look for a long moment so I would never forget. Pale lavender, with deep purple centers trimmed in white. I have never since seen anything to equal it in the flora family. He took out his knife, cutting a stem for me with three orchids on it. They lived for almost two weeks. It was a present I will never forget.

On one of my visits to my parents after I was married, I went downstairs to get the mail. They had a lovely condo in Laguna Hills at that time. I got what was in the mail box. I took the elevator back up; I looked at the letter on top of the bunch, which said, "return ballot in enclosed envelope to The Academy of Arts and Sciences." Daddy took the envelope, throwing it in the trash.

"What is that?" I asked

"It's the ballot for this year's movies."

"Aren't you going to vote?"

"We still go to The Academy Theater twice a week to see the movies, but I don't want to bother with voting."

"Well, can Momma and I look at the things that are up for awards? We'll see which ones we want to vote for?"

"Sure, I don't care."

We got out the ballot. I started picking out the movies we thought should win for best pictures and so forth. If we weren't familiar with the people, we would pick a name we liked. Sometimes we would read ads in the newspaper about someone who was supposed to be really great. We voted for all the women. After we finished voting, we'd put it in the mail, and then we watched the awards to see if our people won.

Usually the most wonderful pictures win, but now you can wonder who was voting for them; it could be Momma, me, or anybody.

My parent's best friends were the Whytocks — Grant and Leota (Ota). They had no children, but her twin sister, Leona (Ona) had a daughter. There was also a third sister named Leora (Ora). Ota's daughter Mary had taken her mother's maiden name. As Mary Carlyle, she was quite well known as a blonde starlet. Mary, her husband, and their son, Jimmy, were all treated as children of Grant, Ota, and Ona. Ona, being a widow, had always lived with Grant and Ota. They were wonderful, talented people. Although

Going to the Academy Theater

```
              THE FOLLOWING NOMINATED FILMS WILL BE SHOWN AT THE
                          DIRECTORS GUILD THEATER
                             7950 Sunset Boulevard
              PLEASE NOTE ALTERNATING SCREENING DATES AND TIMES

                               "THE RIGHT STUFF"
    DATES:        Monday, February 13, 1984      Friday, February 17, 1984
    TIMES:        6:00 P.M.                      9:00 P.M.
    Written and Directed by Philip Kaufman
    Produced by Irwin Winkler and Robert Chartoff
    Unit Production Manager:   David Whorf
    Production Manager:   James D. Brubaker
    1st Assistant Director:   Charles A. Myers
    2nd Assistant Director:   L. Dean Jones Jr.
    Starring:   Sam Shepard, Scott Glenn, Ed Harris, Dennis Quaid
    MPAA Rating:       PG        Running Time:   193. Min.   Print Courtesy of
                                                             Ladd Company

                               "TENDER MERCIES"
    DATES:        Monday, February 13, 1984      Wednesday, February 15, 1984
    TIMES:        10:00 P.M.                     6:00 P.M.
    Directed by Bruce Beresford
    Produced by Philip S. Hobel
    Unit Production Manager:   Tom Joyner
    1st Assistant Director:   Richard Luke Rothschild
    2nd Assistant Director:   Kelly Wimberly
    Starring:   Robert Duvall, Tess Harper
    MPAA Rating:       PG        Running Time:   93 Min.    Print Courtesy of
                                                            Universal Studios

                              "FANNY & ALEXANDER"
    DATES:        Tuesday, February 14, 1984     Wednesday, February 15, 1984
    TIMES:        6:00 P.M.                      8:00 P.M.
    Written and Directed by Ingmar Bergman
    Executive Producer:   Jorn Donner
    Starring:   Pernilla Allwin, Bertil Guve
    MPAA Rating:       R         Running Time:   197 Min.   Print Courtesy of
                                                            Embassy Pictures

                             "TERMS OF ENDEARMENT"
    DATE:         Thursday, February 16, 1984    TIMES:   6:00 and 9:00 P.M.
    Written and Directed by James L. Brooks
    Produced by James L. Brooks
    Unit Production Manager:   Austen Jewell
    1st Assistant Director:   Albert Shaprio
    2nd Assistant Director:   Marty P. Ewing
    Starring:   Debra Winger, Shirley MacLaine, Jack Nicholson, Danny DeVito,
                John Lithgow
    MPAA Rating:       PG        Running Time:   129 Min.   Print Courtesy of
                                                            Paramount Pictures
```

A section of the Academy of Arts and Sciences ballot

they did not have to work, they did because they were too active to do nothing. Ona kept house while Ota and Grant worked, and everyone was happy. They both worked at Edward Small Productions with my daddy.

One night, we went to their house for dinner. Ona was rather upset. She had had a rather harrowing experience that day. Mary and her family went away to Palm Beach. They left their dog in

Ona's care. Well, that is nothing to panic about, but this was no ordinary dog! He was the cocker spaniel that belonged to General MacArthur. He went all over the South Pacific, being sent back to the States when the Philippines were captured.

Ona gave the dog a bath because the general's aide was coming by to see the dog that day. Afterward she tied him to the radiator. He got too hot, catching a cold. That was bad enough because she was petrified he might get pneumonia and die. She called my mother, asking her to come over to help. Mother arrived in a few minutes, because we lived around the corner. She brought nose drops plus other stuff, dosing up the little fellow.

Shortly thereafter the doorbell rang, to reveal an FBI man (he identified himself) asking about the dog. Ona nearly caved in. He asked if she was keeping the dog for Mary, which was his information. He inquired if the dog was well. If she intended to stay at home, he would like to know, because Colonel "so and so" would be by later to visit the dog, as he had been asked by General MacArthur to make sure the dog was all right. Ona ushered Mr. FBI out. When the colonel came, the little dog was feeling fine. With all Mother's attention, he became quite frisky, so the general got a good report. That night at dinner, he was such a sweet dog; he came up to me, kissing my face.

The Whytocks just fit in with our family. They were people like us, ready to try anything that sounded interesting. Before the opening of the beach one year, we went for a ride with them on a Sunday afternoon. Daddy and Grant sat up front. Mama, Ota, and I sat in the back. Ota folded down her backseat card table and the three of us started to play gin rummy. Daddy and Grant were quietly talking.

They turned down Wilshire Boulevard, toward the beach. We rode along. I was torn between looking at the scenery or playing cards. No matter how many times I ride down Wilshire Boulevard, I can never get enough of just plain looking. I was told to keep my mind on the cards. I played, waiting for that wonderful breeze through the open window. However, it never arrived. I looked up to find that Grant had turned the corner. Instead of going down to the beach, he was in

GOING TO THE ACADEMY THEATER

the business section of Santa Monica. We rode around. Finally, he stopped at a used car lot that also sold used trailers.

What were they up to now? There was no telling what they would do next, always counting me in as two extra hands. Their plans, I soon discovered, were that they would buy a trailer hot dog stand, to sell hotdogs on the weekends.

Now really, can you get this picture? Have I conveyed to you this fantastic plan? Let me elaborate: first of all, we were trailer hunting in this, plush, baby blue Cadillac; Grant was Uncle Eddie's associate producer; Daddy was a production manager and business manager for Edward Small Productions; Ota was in the film department. You see, they just needed something to do for the week-

Goldie and Joe with Ota Whytock and her sister Ona

ends. Boy! Mama and Ota were all for it. They even infected me with their enthusiasm. Unfortunately, it never matured. They couldn't find what they were looking for.

This is why, when I see people put on airs, I always wonder what for. The people I know are all people who have "been around." I guess you reach a certain point when you either put on airs or realize how phony they are; you just want most of all to enjoy yourself. Ota's family had its own railroad car when she was a child. When they went with us, she would wear a house dress with a full length mink over it, which you didn't need in California, but she didn't have any other coat, poor thing.

My father was just an ordinary guy. When Uncle Eddie went to Europe to make a picture, Daddy stayed in Hollywood, helping with production of a movie or television series. I'd tell people, Daddy was just home minding the store.

We were a great group for getting together on many occasions. Not only were we many, but with all the cousins, plus additional adopted relatives who were so much a part of the family that nothing went on without them, we were a large gathering.

One night after a session of Bingo (you paid a nickel a card; if you won, you could make a real haul), the men were in the living room. The women migrated to the solarium—with the fountain gone, we could all fit into the room. We started our usual discussions. My cousin, Regina, was the subject, because even though the doctor said she was not expecting a baby, she thought she was. Finally, after several months the doctor said she was expecting; she was very happy because she was already wearing maternity clothes. However, her problem was that she was now in her eleventh month according to her, she still hadn't delivered. We wondered if she ever would, and what she would have when she did.

We talked. Finally, one of the intellectuals around us decided we should discuss state politics. Now, we are all smart. We discussed the pros and cons of each party with their candidates. I was never interested, so I felt like an observer at a tennis match as each side of the group voiced its opinion. Aunt Elsie didn't voice her side of the story. She just sat there with this positive attitude. Whenever there was a break in the conversation, she would lean forward and say, "Vote Republican." The discussion went on.

"Vote Republican," Aunt Elsie said. The conversation got hotter and hotter.

There was another pause, in fact a lull. Everyone had run out of things to say. Taking advantage of the opportunity, Aunt Elsie announced once more, "Vote Republican." This was a great moment in the discussion; no one seemed to know quite what to say to her. They were hung in mid-air by this positive authoritative tone. One of my aunts looked at her, breaking the silence by saying, "Why?"

Aunt Elsie was the "Billie Burke" type. When she was asked "why?" she got all flustered. With all eyes focused upon her, Aunt Elsie threw up her hands, saying "I don't know, but your Uncle Eddie said for me to be sure to tell all of you."

Our Auntie Bea was our aunt by adoption but she was definitely one of us. The most fun was to get her to tell some of her stories.

Going to the Academy Theater

One day Ida Cantor (Eddie Cantor's wife) called her. She asked her to come over that night with Aunt Sara to take out a house guest of Ida's. This woman wanted to go to the opera. Ida and Eddie were busy. Bea said fine. She and Aunt Sara got dressed. Off they went to the Cantors' to get their guest. This lady turned up, greeting them in a long dress, long gloves, and opera glasses. The whole works! Now, she was not really putting on airs, she was just used to the works. She looked at Aunt Bea, then Aunt Sara, who were in slacks (this was in the 1940s) saying, "You're going to the opera like that? You're not dressing?"

They looked at her aghast. "Dressing for us to sit in the third balcony? Not on your life."

Finding no suitable answer to Bea's remarks, off they went, but as the Cantors' guest, the seats were not in the third balcony.

The guest sat between Aunt Sara and Aunt Bea. She was very interested in the opera.

Bea became very bored. ("Who could understand them," she said.)

Bea leaned over to talk to Aunt Sara.

Aunt Sara leaned over to talk to Bea.

Bea leaned over in front of their guest to answer.

Soon they noticed this annoyed the lady so much, Bea did it again just to have fun. The lady didn't like it a bit. This little bit of hokey-pokey went on until the guest could take it no more. Turning to them in a very haughty manner to go with her very proper outfit, she said, "I will never go to the opera with you two again!!"

Bea looked at her saying, "You know what, kid, you got yourself a deal."

When Bea's luck was running, she used to play at the gambling casino at Tijuana, Mexico, for herself and Prince Romanoff. (She took his money.) They used to go down to Mexico quite often. She and Arthur bought a big, expensive car to ride in style, figuring that they would be set for years. Well, styles changed, so there they were with this high and mighty, fancy car when suddenly all her friends were riding in low-slung models. Can't you see her getting an inferiority complex in this big expensive car? All her friends got stiff necks looking up to wave at her as they went by, she said. Nevertheless, their car still held the most people, so they all used to pile into it to ride down to Tijuana to spend the weekend.

One night, they were waiting for Uncle Arthur to take care of the car. Bea saw one of her dear friends, who had recently been widowed. She was playing at one of the tables. Bea had not seen her friend since the lady lost her husband. She was trying to figure out how to express her condolences, well, shall we say, at a gaming table. She pondered over it a bit. Then being straightforward, she walked right up, put her hand on her friend's shoulder, saying, "Polly, I want to tell you how sorry I am about Harry." Polly looked at Bea. She started to cry. She said how terrible it was. "It was just awful." As she sobbed, the tears rolled down her face, ruining her makeup; but I want you to know, as she drowned her sorrow in her handkerchief, Aunt Bea said, she never once missed placing her bet.

About this time, something happened to our dog, Bozo. It's just that it hurts me to tell about it. He was so smart. You know that he wouldn't eat spinach? He'd always take it out of his dish. (Mother thought it was good for his health.) Bozo had had his tonsils removed, but still had a post-nasal drip. He fit right in with the family cause so many of us have asthma or hay fever that my doctor cousin in Beverly Hills had to become a pediatric allergist in self-defense.

Bo had a habit of going up to the grocery store to beg for a bone. (He hated the healthy food he got at home.) No one could refuse him. He should have been in pictures, a real actor. I can't bear to tell you this but one day he got hit by a car. The dog ambulance was called. They rushed him to the hospital, it was to no avail, it was too late. Momma, with tears in her eyes, tried to comfort us with Grandma's old saying, "Life has so many sad occasions, you should never cry over a *hund*." ("dog" in German).

Bo was later replaced by Jeff. Jeff looked exactly like Bo, but that was all. This resemblance prompted Momma to take Jeff to mate him. Dogs in Beverly Hills must be on a leash, but Jeff would have none of that. (Bozo was a special case; he had learned to sneak down the block and back.) If the door was left open just a teeny bit, off Jeff went with everyone in pursuit to heaven only knew where. We didn't want to lose him, too. He tore up plants, wrecked the house, never got housebroken, nothing helped. Everyone loved him because he looked like Bo. Mother used to leave him at the kennel if they went to Palm Springs. She always would ask the vet to please mate Jeff. All she wanted was one puppy out of the litter. This was a great sacrifice, because in Beverly Hills you could get $250 stud fee for a dog with a background, sometimes even more.

Mother asked many times. Finally, the vet said, "Mrs. Small, I don't want to hurt your feelings, but Jeff wouldn't make a very good father. You see...you see...he's psychoneurotic." Well! That's what he said. The outcome of the whole thing was that Jeff ran away. A few days later, the folks found him with a family who had young children. They loved him and he seemed so happy, she gave him to them.

No tears were ever shed over Jeff. Mother switched to cocker spaniels. She had good luck with them. After we all got married, she got females because she always had to outnumber Daddy, so she could have the last word. However, no other dog could take Bo's place in our hearts.

Miriam, my older sister, was married, living in Alabama. Because she was expecting, the doctor advised her to come home. We were sorry she had to leave her husband, but she was better off with us in California.

What a family we made. Elinor was twelve, a difficult age. I worried over Herman, over Miriam because she was pregnant and very sick with asthma. Miriam worried about her husband, worried about me worrying about her and Herman, pretending not to worry about herself, even though she felt terrible.

Mother was a nervous wreck trying to keep all of us happy. Daddy was trying to keep Mother happy. They slept in the back bedroom with their bathroom next to them. Elinor and I slept in the middle bedroom that shared a bathroom with Miriam who slept in the front bedroom. For six months, Mother ran through our room whenever she heard a noise from Miriam. I didn't get much sleep. We swore the night Miriam was to go to the hospital that Mother would sleep. No, not her, she vowed. No one in our family had had a baby since Elinor had been born.

One night about 4:00, I was awakened by the smell of cigarette smoke. I saw a light under the bathroom door. I waited for mother to go swooshing by. She didn't show. I tiptoed into the bathroom. There was Miriam, puffing away on a cigarette, talking on the phone to the doctor, making plans to go to the hospital. I went to the kitchen to get a glass of water with medicine for her. We packed her things. Mama slept through it all. Not a peep from her. I can still see us at 5:00 a.m. tiptoeing in to get her. We stood in the doorway, "Momma, Daddy," we called.

No answer. "MOMMA, DADDY!" we called again.

Finally, Mother sputtered and started waving her arms around, "What's, what's, what's the matter?"

"Miriam is ready. She has to go to the hospital."

"Why didn't you call me? Sweetheart, get up. Miriam is ready. We've got to go."

Daddy got up. Mother started rushing around like crazy.

At 6:00 a.m., they dashed out to the car.

We helped them in. Daddy pressed down on the starter. He pressed down again. He turned the key on, next off. Mother started insisting to let her drive, but it was dead; nothing, no response. We helped them all out again. We called my cousin, Regina. She was thrilled. She would rush right over.

Mother rushed inside to call the Automobile club. As she did, she slammed her finger in the car door. The AAA, followed by my cousin, came at the same time. After getting Daddy's car started, we helped them all in again. My cousin followed in case they ran into any more trouble.

After they left, Elinor and I collapsed from excitement on the sofa. I was scared stiff. I'd never seen anyone in labor before. Would they get there in time? Would she be all right? We heard a fire siren. I told Elinor, trying to calm her, that maybe the siren was not a fire. Maybe it was someone going to the hospital in an ambulance to have a baby, just like Miriam. That didn't make a hit with her at all. She turned her mature twelve-year-old face toward me, saying with real disgust, "If it was an ambulance coming for me, I'd wish it was a fire."

What do you do at 6:00 a.m. when you've been up half the night with a woman in labor? (She behaved fine, of course, but I was a wreck.) You're nervous as a result. You're trying to keep a youngster from worrying, too. I knew I couldn't go back to sleep. I tried to think of something else that would help Mother, please her, and get us busy right away. I turned to Elinor who, now fully awake and realizing the seriousness of the situation, was beginning to look worried.

I said, "I know. I've got it. Let's vacuum!" And at 6:00 a.m. we went to get the Hoover and that is exactly what we did.

My Cousin Bobby Small

My father Joseph's brother, Eddie, had a son, Bobby. As I said, Uncle Eddie ran away from home when he was twelve. He went to New York, then to Hollywood, where he became a movie producer. His son Bobby was brought up in the lap of luxury in Beverly Hills with chauffeur-driven limousines, maids, and cooks, before the war, WWII. He was about 5'3" like the rest of the men in our family; he had red hair (like his father as a child) and freckles.

Bobby went to private schools. His mother (Aunt Elsie) told about the time she went to pick him up at school in the limousine. Seeing him on the front lawn of the school, she rolled down the window and called to him. Bobby turned his back to her. One of the other kids said: "Bobby, that lady is calling you."

Bobby Small and his mother, my Aunt Elsie

He looked at the other kid, saying, "I never saw her before in my life." That describes his personality.

He was not one to be an important person, just a plain guy. He played extras in some of his father's movies, especially the cowboy ones, and that's what he became — a cowboy.

One time my sisters and I went with our husbands to the Palladium. They had valet parking. We pulled up for the car to be parked. There was my cousin Bobby, who was the valet parking man.

The inside of the club had a huge dance floor with tables surrounding it and a large stage where famous bands played. I think Artie Shaw was there then. Our conversation that night was if we should tip Bobby, since his father owned the place. We did offer him money, but he refused to take it.

Bobby never went to college, but joined the cavalry in the U.S. Army. He was sent to Lincoln, Nebraska, where he worked with horses, which he loved. Most people do not know that the government had a cavalry then, but there was one. He met his wife there. After the war, they lived around the corner from my family in Beverly Hills. On my day off on the weekends, I used to walk over to spend the day with his wife, Gloria, who was pregnant at the time. They were close to my parents, staying in touch over the years.

He bought his first ranch in Solvang, California, raising horses and cattle. Bobby needed to buy a house trailer for whoever would work for him. My father went with him because Daddy had to okay the deal. Years later his ranch became Edwards Air Force Base.

Bobby and his family

One time he came into the studio for Daddy to go over his books with him for the accountant. He walked in the office with a brown paper bag, and handed it to my father. Those were his records. One receipt from the general store was for ten dollars, three for cigarettes and seven dollars cash, because he didn't have any money. He always had people who accommodated him.

I remember another day as I was walking into the Beverly Wilshire Hotel, to go somewhere with my Aunt Elsie. Bobby was walking in ahead of me. The doorman, who was dressed like a South American general, opened the door for Bobby, who had on jeans, a plaid shirt, and mud-caked boots. Bowing, the doorman said, "Good morning Mr. Small," to which Bobby answered, "Hello, Jose."

When my sister Elinor got married, Bobby and Gloria came to their wedding as did the rest of the California family and friends. It wasn't a formal affair, but you wouldn't have known that my cousin Bobby was a horse and cattle farmer. He had on a suit that had to have cost many hundreds of dollars. When he pulled out a gold cigarette lighter, just the way he did it made you know he was a man of means. That night he called his neighbor to tell him he would take his cow to town the next day if the guy would do something for him. That same day at the wedding Bobby asked his father (Uncle Eddie) if he could have the station wagon that was at their house in Palm Springs. Uncle Eddie said yes because no one was using it but the help. Bobby was thrilled. (This was one of the cars given to the studio during the war, and civilians were unable to get cars.)

He and his family eventually returned to Lincoln. In the winter when it began to snow, Bobby would go out on one of the horses or one of their trucks to round up the horses and cattle they owned. Gloria got into their car or station wagon, put their baby in a laundry basket on the seat, with a rifle by her side, and helped round up all the animals. She was just a shy blonde girl, but nothing was too much for her.

Bobby liked to dance. In later years he went out every night to do so. His wife never went with him. He asked Gloria for a divorce, moving out of the house into a trailer on the ranch they owned at that time. When Uncle Eddie died in L.A. in 1977, the funeral had to wait because Bobby had not hooked up a phone on the remote areas of the expansive property. His family had to go out to tell him the news. It was further delayed because Bobby didn't fly, having to go to California by other means.

He eventually got some form of cancer. When he was dying, Gloria went to the hospital to stay with him until he died. She always loved him. She eventually married a man who worked for them training horses. I think Bobby asked for a divorce so she could marry this man and he would take care of her. Money was no problem. When he died, Gloria called me asking: "He really did love me, didn't he?"

They had four children, who are all grown, with their own children. Their son was called "Pinky" because he had his father's red hair. Gloria wrote and sent pictures. I'm sorry to say I lost touch because I was ill the last time she wrote. I have been negligent to look her up on my computer.

My Uncle Eddie

My Uncle Eddie ran away to New York at age twelve and went into the theatrical agency business at fifteen, getting jobs for actors and actresses on the stage.

Edward Small

The Small Company Theatrical Agency later became a subsidiary of Edward Small Productions, when Uncle Eddie had starting making movies in 1906.

Uncle Eddie decided what he wanted to produce, who would star in the movie or television show, supervising all. My uncle made 359 movies and many, many TV shows. A few of them are: *Lassie, Fury, The Story of a Horse,* and *The Halls of Ivy* with Ronald Coleman, *The Last of the Mohicans* with J. Carrol Naish, and several Bob Hope movies. The most well-known movie was *Witness for the Prosecution* with Tyrone Power and Marlene Dietrich, which was nominated for an Academy Award.

This story is based on some things my father told me about his brother. The rest is from an unpublished autobiography by my uncle, Edward Schmalheiser, known as Edward Small in the business, where he made a name for himself. I was always amazed that he never legally changed his name.

He tells in his book that he went up to the Catskills to get a job in the hotels as a singer and dancer. The season did not open

My Uncle Eddie

From Lassie, *produced by Edward Small*

until later in the year, so he tried to get a job for room and board to survive. The people there were German. They said, "If you're Jewish, don't stay around here. Jews don't belong here." This was in the early 1900s; the Germans were always that way, even when they moved to the USA. So that's why Uncle Eddie called himself Eddie Small. Ironically, the Catskills became a favorite vacation spot for New York Jews.

In Grandpa's roofing business in Savannah, his sons were supposed to help. Although Morris was the eldest son, Eddie was the one expected to help his father. Uncle Morris couldn't help grandpa because he always had a runny nose. My grandparents thought it was a cold, but I think it was probably allergy.

Uncle Eddie was the one who at five had to climb up a ladder to the top of a building, sometimes a couple of stories high in Savannah, with a bucket of nails or a bucket of hot coals for soldering a tin roof. Uncle Eddie would be afraid to climb down, so Grandpa would throw a hammer at him to make him go back for other things. Born in 1891, he persuaded my grandmother to say he was six years old when he was still five, so he could go to school, getting away from my grandfather and the roofing business.

He went to school at five, going to the only public school in Savannah, on Bull and Oglethorpe, in the fall of 1896. The school was across the street from the Savannah Theater. Today that school building holds the Board of Education. The theater has been in use continually since then. He became fascinated by the acting, skipping school all the time to go over there. He was taught how to sing, dance and tell jokes by the porter, who took care of the building.

Uncle Eddie would deliver flyers all over town for a free ticket to the shows, which came to Savannah. He kept getting expelled from school for skipping and going over to the theater. The principal got the Catholic school to accept him, but the priests sent him back. Nothing could keep him away from the show business. He practiced singing, dancing, and learning the timing of telling jokes. You have to realize he was very tiny; he never was any taller than 5'3" as an adult. Picture this: a young boy not even five feet tall with red hair and freckles, dancing and singing "Hello, My Baby,"and "Turkey in the Straw," telling jokes in between.

When the porter thought he was ready, he got Uncle Eddie singing jobs in churches and other places. His payment was ice cream. He was happy because there was never any of that at his house. He was thrilled with the chance to perform, being chosen to dance and sing in a show given to raise money for the veterans of the Civil War. He was a great success, which cemented his desire to be in show business. He often put on shows in the neighborhood using my father, his sisters, and anybody he could find to participate or come to see them.

Hollywood Producer

EDWARD SMALL
Savannahian, who is producer of "My Son, My Son," and who is rated as Hollywood's outstanding independent producer.

Uncle Eddie made it his business to get out of Savannah as soon as he could. Would you believe at the age of seven, he went with a traveling group of actors, leaving permanently at twelve? Shortly after the Veterans' Benefit show, a stage group came to town. They were in dire straits because the ingénue in their show was sick, and they needed someone immediately. Uncle Eddie was asked to fill in. He went home to ask his parents, thinking his mother would say all right, but his father would have a fit. Just the opposite happened. His mother got terribly upset, but his father said, "Let him go. He'll be a bum, just like the rest of the bums." So he went, at seven years old where he found more

My Uncle Eddie

affection and friendship than he had ever found before with family or friends. He did the child's part. Also, during the changes of costumes and scenery, he would sing, dance, and tell jokes. He traveled with the group until they couldn't draw audiences any more. Since there was no more money, one of the ladies collected enough pocket change to buy him a ticket home.

He wasn't too anxious to be there. Grandpa wasn't too anxious to see him, either. Can you imagine, at seven years old?

He was made to go to school, but in the afternoon he got a job, that way he didn't have to help Grandpa. He ran errands for a food warehouse. He took his money home to Grandma, whom he loved very much. He never did get along with Grandpa, but the truth is that of all his siblings, who were all sweet like my grandma, he was the only one just like his father.

He managed to do shows after work, sometimes getting some odd jobs at the theater. He saved some money that he didn't take home to Grandma. At twelve years old he wrote a letter of farewell to his mother, dropped it in the mailbox, went to the train station, bought a half-price ticket to New York.

His boss at the Savannah food warehouse had given him a letter of recommendation to a friend in New York, who was a theatrical agent. Uncle Eddie went to work for him as an office boy. He eventually quit, getting another job as a "call boy."

At The Astor Hotel in the early 1900s when someone in the theater business was staying in the hotel or eating lunch there and got a phone call, they would have to go where the phone was located. So Uncle Eddie, who had a loud voice, went around in a uniform saying, "Call for Mr. Barrymore," or someone else. He got a small salary, sometimes getting tipped ten cents. He got to meet a lot of famous people. This allowed him to use their help later in the theatrical agency he opened at fifteen, because they remembered him.

When he died in the 1970s, his secretary gave his unpublished autobiography to my father, telling him to give it to me, so I could see about getting it published. It's absolutely incredible. What I write here is quoted from his own words in the manuscript.

From Savannah to Hollywood

Between the age of twelve and fifteen, he put a Wild West show together with another fellow. They traveled in upstate New York. When the show failed, they escaped just ahead of the law, going to Staten Island, living in an unoccupied beach cottage. They survived by eating raw clams they dug up on the beach. When they found someone by phone who would lend them money to pay the actors from their show, plus whatever other bills they had accrued, they went back to New York City to start over.

Uncle Eddie, at the age of fifteen, became an agent for the stage and vaudeville, and also a theatrical agent for the movies. He decided to charge actors five percent of their salary for every job he got for them. He started interviewing as many of them as he could, becoming very successful.

Uncle Eddie with ads for an Elvis Presley movie

He did many inventive things, representing actors, directors, musicians, and writers by the dozens. He placed very famous leading ladies, men, or character actors in jobs in the entertainment business.

Uncle Eddie stayed in New York for many years as a theatrical agent, making his own movies. Eventually he moved the agency to Los Angeles under the care of Uncle Morris. It was on Sunset Boulevard.

Uncle Eddie has his own star on Hollywood Boulevard. When he died, he left money for wings for the Cedars of Lebanon Hospital, the Cedars of Sinai Hospital, and the Motion Picture Retirement Home.

My Uncle Eddie

Uncle Eddie's star on Hollywood Boulevard

Joseph and Goldie Small (right) at the dedication of the Motion Picture Retirement Home wing to Edward Small

Going to Lunch with Aunt Elsie

One Saturday in the midst of World War II, I was at home in California. No college or work that day. I was just sitting on the sofa in the den reading the latest novel; I wasn't even going to take a shower.

The phone rang. "Get that," Momma yelled from her bedroom. I really didn't want to, because I knew it meant either their friends the Whytocks would want to go on one of their excursions with Momma and Daddy, or Aunt Elsie wanting to go to lunch. Since I didn't have anything to do, it meant I would either have to go with them or my mother would give me some chore at home. When I picked up the phone, it was Aunt Elsie saying she'd pick us up for lunch at noon.

Aunt Elsie and Uncle Eddie lived in the Beverly Wilshire Hotel on Wilshire Boulevard and Rodeo Drive, across the street from the Brown Derby, a famous restaurant where all the movie stars went. That's where we usually went with her to eat lunch.

"Go take your shower, get dressed. You're not going to lie around here all day," Momma said. I got up, went in my bedroom, pulling out a party dress. Going to lunch with Aunt Elsie was a real dress-up affair. I took my shower, washed my hair, put polish on my fingernails. I got out my favorite high heel yellow leather shoes with the pocketbook to match. The dress I wore was pale green with little yellow flowers embroidered on it. After I got ready, I went to sit in the living room, waiting to be picked up.

Aunt Elsie had a big house in Beverly Hills. When the war started, people couldn't get help to maintain a big house or limousine. Aunt Elsie and Uncle Eddie moved into the Beverly Wilshire Hotel, where they had an apartment. They had help from the hotel.

Going to Lunch With Aunt Elsie

Besides that, they had a fellow who was their butler and chauffeur, cooking breakfast or whatever other meals they wanted to eat in their apartment. The limousine they had before the war was at my uncle's movie studio up on blocks (to cut the price of insurance).

The Ford Motor Company gave Edward Small Productions four automobiles every year for one dollar each, to use in movies or television series (like *Lassie*). The cars they got during the war had to be kept longer than a year because the automobile companies were making vehicles for the government. The ones they had from Ford for the duration of the war were a fancy Lincoln, a station wagon, a Mustang, and a four-door sedan.

Uncle Eddie drove the Lincoln, my father drove the Mustang, the station wagon was used on the set wherever they were shooting, or sometimes at their house in Palm Springs. Aunt Elsie got to use the little four-door sedan, which was a pretty sky blue. The three of us being helped in and out of a Ford sedan by the chauffeur in front of the Brown Derby was like a scene out of a Jack Benny show. But there was a war going on, so a person had to make do, the best he could.

Uncle Eddie had been married first to a woman the family never met. When they got a divorce, he gave her a million dollars. Later he married Aunt Elsie.

I loved my Aunt Elsie. She had been a chorus girl in New York when my uncle met her. She was beautiful and sweet. She had a son, Bud, by a first marriage, but Elsie and Eddie only had Bobby.

This particular Saturday, the doorbell rang. There stood Joe, the chauffeur, in his uniform, to pick us up. He seated me in the front passenger seat, putting Momma in the back. He said Aunt Elsie wasn't quite ready, so he had offered to get us first. We rode down Olympic Boulevard going to Beverly Drive. He turned the car so the passenger side faced the front door of the hotel, and Aunt Elsie could get in easily that way. After she was seated in the car, he made a U-turn ending up at the front door of the Brown Derby, which was across the street.

From Savannah to Hollywood

Since everyone knew my aunt, we were seated at the most desirable table there. The menu was brought, the specials told. They had things nobody ever saw or heard of in Savannah. They had salads with watercress, octopus, artichokes, exotic fruits, avocado, vegetables, and greens that were simply amazing. The rolls were larger than one's fist, smelling of all kinds of herbs, served with delicious jams and jellies. We had some kind of wild English tea. I remember my mother telling me that when you stir your tea, you don't hit the sides of the cup with your spoon.

The Brown Derby

While we waited for our lunch, Aunt Elsie would tell me who different people were. A lot of them were her friends, who came over to speak. All were people in the producing side of the industry, but some actors, too. One man's name was John Smith, but I never remembered his name when I saw him in a movie. Tourists were whispering to each other, wondering who we were. Momma acted important, which was easy for her. Aunt Elsie *was* important. I just sat there in amazement, as always.

That day Aunt Elsie had on a spectacular bracelet. It was about two inches wide with stones completely surrounding her wrist. It had blocks of diamonds and rubies. As I admired it, she took it off, telling me to put it on. I asked her how many stones there were. She said she didn't know, to count them, which I did. There were four squares with thirty-six stones in each. It had a square of diamonds, a square of rubies, etc. The stones were really large, at least a half-carat each, and they all matched.

After lunch the dessert wagon came to our table. Everything looked too beautiful to eat. I remember chocolate, chocolate, and chocolate. Even as a child I could never eat rich things, so I opted for sherbet with their grapefruit cake, for which they were famous.

GOING TO LUNCH WITH AUNT ELSIE

After we finished eating, Joe came to get us, we went for a ride around Beverly Hills.

None of us wanted to go shopping. It was in the days before credit cards, but picture me, eighteen years old from the Deep South, going to buy something in Saks Fifth Avenue. Aunt Elsie decided she needed to take me to meet her furrier in Beverly Hills. Of course I pretended that was what I wanted to do.

Uncle Eddie and Aunt Elsie with their family

When we arrived, we were ushered into a lush room with a wall which opened up to make the room twice its size. I tried on different jackets. Momma and Aunt Elsie decided on a white fox jacket for me. When the saleslady went to get the alteration person, Momma said she would pay for it. I could pay her back on the installment plan. The sleeves were too long. The coat would be fixed. I was to pick it up later.

The following week I went to pick up my coat. I had really gone "Hollywood" by this time. My hair was long and blonde. I was going out, socializing a lot, so I was just in the need of a little fur jacket. Although you didn't need one in L.A. — a blonde coat to match my hair — everyone had one, my dear.

I could hear someone moving around in the salon next to us. She sneezed.

I said, "God bless you."

She giggled. Then she thanked me.

I waited and waited.

Finally the lady came back, saying to me, "I'm sorry to keep you waiting, Miss Small, but Norma Shearer is in the next room, she has your coat on. She wants to buy one just like it. As soon as I can get her to take it off, I'll I bring it to you."

"Oh that's all right," I breathed.

A couple of minutes later, Norma Shearer walked in wearing my coat.

"Miss Small," she said, "please let me shake your hand. I'm so very glad to meet you. Do you know if it were not for your Uncle Eddie, I would not be where I am today? He believed in me in New York. He gave me my first important role. I owe everything to him."

"I'm glad to meet you, too," I said.

I introduced Aunt Elsie and then Momma. Miss Shearer was pleased to meet them, too.

"I love your coat. I plan to get a full-length one just like it. Do you think it looks all right on me?"

Norma Shearer

I certainly did.

She got a full-length one just like mine. My coat died long ago. I wonder what happened to hers.

I wore my coat on all my dates.

Another time I went with Aunt Elsie alone. She took me to the Christian Science Church. She was born Jewish, but joined that church. After the service, people got up, giving testimonies, including my aunt. I don't remember what she said, but the lady next to me turned to her friend on the other side saying, "That's Mrs. Small, she used to be Jewish." Oh, well.

Arthur's Proposal and Our Wedding

Meanwhile, back in Savannah, Herman's Uncle Arthur had just returned from Italy. Arthur wrote to the family in Savannah all about how he had gone to visit Herman at his base. How terrible it was that Herman had not returned from his last mission.

After spending his leave in Savannah, Arthur was being sent to Riverside, California. As he got ready to leave, Herman's father asked him to come to see me in Los Angeles. He told him to take me out to some fancy place and to ask me to marry Herman. Arthur just couldn't believe this was for real. After being convinced that this was the thing to do, he agreed, but thought it was a wild idea. He was shy, but thank heavens he was sent to speak for Herman. (Herman never did ask me to marry him until we were married fifty years, when we were married again to celebrate.)

Herman's Uncle Arthur

The phone rang at my uncle's office one day when I was operating the switchboard. A familiar voice said, "It's Arthur, I'm in town. I would like to take you to dinner."

"*Moi?*" I thought. There must be some mistake. Arthur was Herman's uncle but with only a few years difference, they were more like brothers.

Hearing Arthur's voice, I thought, Herman's daddy put him up to this. That was true. Arthur had always been a "BTO" (Big Time Operator) in Savannah. For him to take me out was something. However, I took it in stride because I was not the little girl with the hayseed in her ears any more, or so I thought. I accepted it with only the slightest bit of wonderment.

Arthur came to pick me up at the Small Company at five p.m. When he walked in the door in his uniform, he looked so like Herman, I felt weak. Herman and Arthur look more alike than any two members of their family. Their hands are the same, also their physiques. Arthur has the same mannerisms. He even wrinkles his shoes the same way. Arthur took me to the Garden of Allah hotel for a drink. Then we went sightseeing in Beverly Hills.

Afterward he took me home to dress. The folks were so happy to see him. My sister, Miriam, kept shaking her head. When we left, she told Mother that it was very strange for Arthur to take me out. We went to the Coconut Grove, in the Ambassador Hotel, for dinner that evening.

Ambassador Hotel

If I neglect to report the conversation, it is because Arthur didn't say much. He had a job to do that he was very nervous about. I just jabbered on. I don't remember what I said, but the people at the next table found it interesting. They listened all evening. The tables for two were so close, you could eat from the plates at the next table.

We ate our dinner. Always eat first if you have a job to do, in my husband's family. We talked about Savannah news. We danced a while. Arthur told me he had something to tell me about Herman.

My heart turned over. "Something has happened to him. I knew it. I knew it," I thought. We returned to our table. "No,"

Arthur's Proposal and Our Wedding

Arthur said, "I mean I want to ask you something about Herman."

No, he wasn't nervous, just petrified. Here I'd always thought he was such a man about town. Just goes to show you. Arthur's wheels started to grind. Honestly, you can just see his and Herman's brains working when they get ready to answer. I waited frantically. The wheels went *grrrrrrr*.

However, by this time, I was a wreck. "Yes...yes...yes?"

Then Arthur said to me, "Philip (Herman's father) wants to know if Herman comes back, will you marry him?"

I remember Freddie Martin's orchestra was playing "Candy."

I pretended to think about it for a moment. After all, this was the biggest moment of my life so far. The people at the next tables leaned forward waiting expectantly for my answer. Arthur turned twenty different colors.

I acted as if I were thinking very hard. After a moment I answered, "Yes, oh yes!"

"Well, don't you have to go ask your mother and daddy?" he asked. I didn't want to start laughing at such a serious moment. I was really glad he had come to ask me, because the night before I had been thinking, "What if Herman never comes back?" I felt this void, as if part of me would always be missing.

"No." I started to cry. They were still playing "Candy." I wanted so much to remember the words so I could sing it for Herman. He still doesn't know which song it was, because he was a prisoner, and he never heard it. Arthur was even more upset than I was. Still red, he said, "I've never asked anyone to get married before. I feel as if I asked you myself."

"A girl usually gets kissed when she gets engaged. Aren't you going to kiss me?" Ah... how innocent I was. Arthur just wanted to die. He leaned over, kissing me on the cheek. Everyone around was very pleased and leaned back in their chairs with a real sense of satisfaction.

We went downstairs in the Ambassador Hotel to call my folks. I don't remember a word they said. Well, I do remember something about "happy" and "come home now." Before we left, we sent Herman's folks a telegram. The telegram said, "Helen said yes.

From Savannah to Hollywood

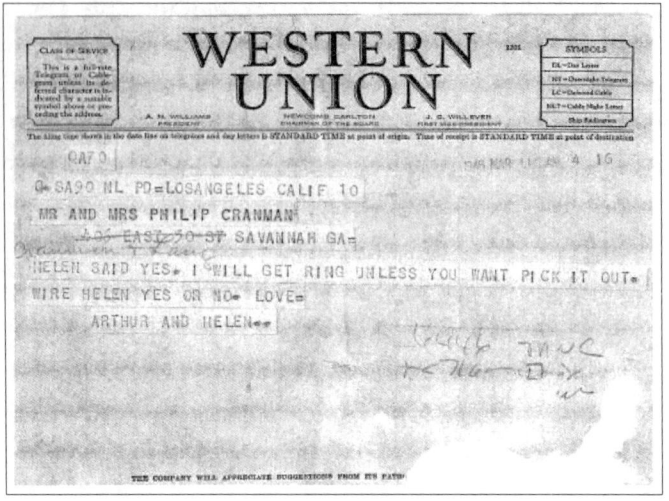

Will you get the ring or should I?" The lady at the telegraph desk had the starriest look in her eyes. I was crying. Arthur was so ... embarrassed. The lady said she thought we made a lovely couple.

He took me home. My folks greeted us at the door with a mixture of excitement, wonderment, confusion, but most of all, happiness. I was just confused. It was a rather strange situation. We were all so excited. My parents considered me the flighty one. They were so worried that I would never grow up to be ready for marriage. Well, I just wanted Herman to come back. Let it be soon. This happened in March.

The next day, two dozen American Beauty roses arrived with the card, "Herman would want you to have these, I'm sure. Love, Arthur." I still have that card.

I wanted Herman to bring me the ring. That way, it

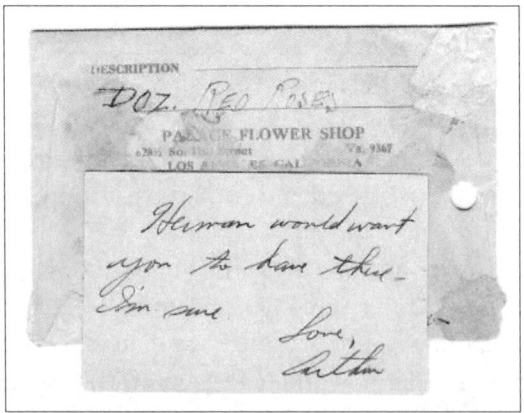

Arthur's Proposal and Our Wedding

seemed to make it sure he would return. He would have to come back, making the final moment his. I could not take a ring from anyone but him. I sat down that day and wrote him the only real love letter I'd ever written. The paper is yellow, the envelope is brown, but the words are the same:

> My Dearest Sweet Herman:
>
> I have written many letters to you in the past few months. They have all been letters to keep up your morale. To let you know that I was here, that I did care. This letter is for you to read when you come home so that you'll know exactly how I feel. Then if you still want me, I am yours for always. It took me a long time to realize how very deep my love is for you. Not that I wasn't conscious of it, but you have been my whole life all my life. I never thought of being without you. Now that I realize I might have to spend the rest of my life without you or perhaps find someone else, I know that I could never do such a thing. I could never give you up for any reason, because you are the other half of me that makes me a person, a good person, a happy person. I want to tell you all the reasons that make me love you. I love you cause you're good. So good that it hurts. I love you 'cause I just do. I love the color of your hair, the texture of it, like little feathers. I love your green eyes and dark skin. Your smooth clean face, your beautiful teeth. You are so tall and your hands I would like to paint for their beauty. Your walk is grace. All the wonderful things that make you, you.
>
> I know we both will have changed. We will have to learn to know each other all over again. Perhaps there are changes that will only make us more grown up. If you understand how much I really do care, when you read this you will put your arms around me, holding me tight so I will know.
>
> All my love always.
> Helen

I had a map of Europe on the back of my bedroom door. Every day I marked off the progress of General Patton's army. I kept writing, hoping Herman would get my letters, but he never did. Even though we hadn't heard from him in a long time, I just knew he would be all right.

From Savannah to Hollywood

One day in May, I was home from work. I was at my dressing table combing my hair. Suddenly I started to tremble and felt weak in the knees. I stopped to think, "What day is it? What time is it? I must ask Herman if he was thinking of me on this day at this hour." I ran to the radio. You could get news twenty-four hours in Los Angeles. I turned it on. I waited impatiently for it to warm up. It started to hum. The first words to come out of the radio were: "50,000 Allied prisoners of war were liberated at Moosberg, Germany, today." It was April 9, 1945.

I didn't need to hear any more. All of us cried that day. We talked back and forth to Savannah. Although we still had no official word, we knew Herman was supposed to be either in Moosberg or Nuremberg. So we could only hope and pray, because we still did not know what condition he would be in. With all we learned later, it is truly a miracle.

A few weeks later, we opened the newspaper. There was a picture of the arrival of some liberated American prisoners landing in Boston. The nurse, staying with us to help Miriam with her baby, said she bet Herman was on that boat. Shortly thereafter the phone rang. It was a long distance operator asking for me. She asked me to please keep the line open for a call. I got all excited. I knew Herman's folks had heard from the War Department.

The operator kept me on the phone because she kept saying my party was still busy on the wire. I knew that Herman's parents must have put in a call for me. They probably were calling so many other people, and people were calling them. I sat waiting for forty-five minutes.

The operator kept calling to see if our line was open. Finally, she tied it up completely. She kept telling me not to dare go away from the phone. I wondered who it was in Savannah at the telephone company who was just as excited as I was. Finally, she got back on the phone. She told me she was sorry for the delay but my party had been talking for forty-five minutes. I waited to hear my future in-laws' voices on the phone.

Suddenly, the operator said: "Miss Small, I have Lieutenant Cranman for you, calling from Boston."

Arthur's Proposal and Our Wedding

"Go ahead, please. Go ahead, please." Herman had put in calls for his parents and for me, and had been talking to his folks. As I write this, I remember I had chills with tears streaming down my face as I heard his voice over the phone,

I asked how he was, if he was unharmed. In his usual calm way, he said he was fine. Everyone said he might be affected by his treatment, but he sounded wonderful. Little did I know that after he bailed out, he had been chained, had a gun put to his head, marched through the streets, threatened with pitch forks, put in solitary confinement; then months later, taken on a march in forty below zero weather, until his feet were frozen, eating only food the prisoners could carry. How can one say in a few lines, "301 days of prison camp"? He is the one with the story to tell. He says in his usual assured manner that he is all in one piece. He did not give life or limb, he was not treated like the people on Bataan. He is right. He is the most fine, honorable man I know or have ever known. Somehow, without even making an effort, he is very close to G-d always.

Back to that moment on the phone long ago, Herman said he talked to his folks. I asked if they told him about us. I guess he misunderstood me because he said yes. Later on in the conversation I learned they had not. They just told him to be sure to get the call through to me.

Daddy kept yelling, asking if Herman knew we were engaged. That is the only time in our lives we told Daddy to "please shut up."

I asked Herman to tell me he loved me. He did so but he did sound a little strange.

Finally, Mother got on the phone and in a buoyant manner said, "Hello, son, how does it feel to be engaged?"

"Engaged? Are we engaged?"

Herman was rather stunned. He said he met one of our friends, Bubba Horovitz, on the boat when they were returning from Europe. Bubba had congratulated him on being engaged. Herman told him he was mistaken. However, as Bubba had not been a prisoner, he had the news right, it was no mistake.

It was a little late, but I wondered if he really wanted me. He talked to everyone in my family, saying he would call later about the wedding plans and then we hung up. Later he told me he went to his bunk in a complete state of shock and just stayed there.

Plans were made to get married in Beverly Hills at our house. Just the family planned to come. Herman arrived the day before the wedding. We all went down to the station to meet him and his mother. Hundreds of people came pouring into the station from the train.

Suddenly I saw him, tall and straight, over the heads of all the other people. He looked fine. He had lost some weight. He had a slight nervous twitch, which was small enough a price to pay for what he had been through. I was so relieved. All I could think was, "Thank you, G-d. Thank you so much." He was just as beautiful as ever. He took me for a ride in his Uncle Arthur's car, which Arthur left for us to use. I showed Herman the way down to the beach. I can still feel his arms around me. It was a particular moment that will always seem different from the rest. He took out a box. You know, the kind rings come in. He opened it, the light struck the stone. It was beautiful. I was so happy that I had waited for him to put it on my finger.

The family came the day before the wedding to inspect all my clothes, my ring, and Herman. That day was June 16, Daddy's fiftieth birthday. He kept walking around all day saying, "A man's only fifty once in his life. I'll never be fifty again. Nobody even cares. Sweetheart, it's my birthday." Sweetheart was just too busy, though. We did care, however.

That same day Momma told Herman, "I tried to make a lady out of her. Now, she's your problem." (She didn't fail. It was that I was like my father, walking to the beat of my own drum.) My mother asked him if he still wanted to go through with the whole thing, since he had been more or less been railroaded into it. He said yes, just glad Arthur had spoken for him. I am too, because I wonder if he would ever have gotten up the courage. Once he married me, like all men, he is the ruler of the roost now. At least, he's got me thinking he is.

The day came for the wedding. Relatives started arriving early. Everyone was quite at home. Herman and his mother arrived. I was

Arthur's Proposal and Our Wedding

rushed into my room so I wouldn't see him. Everyone outside my bedroom was enjoying themselves. I was supposed to rest. While in my room, I thought back to the day when I was five and Herman was six. How I used to sit on his doorstep waiting for him to come out to play with me, but he never did.

The hour arrived. I wore an aqua silk dress with an aqua tulle hat. Herman looked magnificent in his tan uniform. The ceremony was short, quick, but very nice. My sisters were my attendants. A friend of ours from Savannah was Herman's best man. I couldn't wait for the ceremony to be over. The rabbi couldn't, either. Lots of other people were getting married that day. Only a little time was allotted for each ceremony.

We left on our wedding trip. We heard the family stayed at Momma's all day, and most of the night. We had a lovely time on our honeymoon. We got the broken bed. The hotel had been looking months for it. All the lovely things that happen to honeymooners were in store for us.

After a few months more of the Air Force, we went back to Savannah to live. That's where we've been ever since.

Back in Savannah

Who Are You?

In this country, it's not so much who you are, but what you have accomplished. Almost everyone who came to live in the United States did so because they had to leave their own country. If a person tells you how many generations his family has been here, it's because they had to leave Europe earlier or were smart enough to get out when there was serious trouble beginning to appear.

I write from a Jewish point of view, but this reasoning goes for all people who immigrated here. There was much anti-Semitism all over Europe. The Holocaust was one of the worst. Let's not forget the Spanish Inquisition in the 1400s!

In the 19th century, Jewish families were required to have one son serve in the Russian army for twenty years, so many of them left in whatever manner they could. Sometimes the father would come to this country first, sending for the rest of the family one by one.

This was approximately the last half of the 1800s to early 1900s and later. The ships were wood sailing ships or steam vessels or a combination of the two until around the beginning of the twentieth century when they started using metal ships with turbine engines. Many came in the ships' steerage, which meant traveling in terrible conditions.

If you were ill when you got here, they sent you back.

Many people came through Ellis Island in New York, although some people came to different ports, such as Boston, Philadelphia, Canada, or Savannah. They even came to ports further south, like New Orleans. Their ports in Europe were from England, France, and Germany. Lots of people came to their ports of embarkation from Odessa, Russia.

Some came by train, but my husband's grandmother said they walked from Odessa to Le Havre, France, with all their possessions in a single push cart. When they got to France, someone stole the push cart. They lost everything except a money belt Grandpa Cranman had around his waist. They came aboard a ship going to Canada, where they lived until they came into this country. Most people came with very little and it wasn't until after the First World War that the more prosperous folks got out with their belongings and money.

My knowledge of why different ethnic groups came here is limited. The Irish came because of the potato famine, English for religious freedom. The British populated some of this country with debtors and criminals. When the Revolutionary War started, the British couldn't send them to this country anymore, so they sent those people to Australia.

> Savannah's start was to be that of an import port for human flesh. Founder Oglethorpe figured on settling the "debatable land" between the Savannah and Altamaha rivers with prisoners of debtors jails from England.
>
> Indeed, the new colonies of America were seen as a possible well, haven for English criminals of all classes until a little thing called the Revolutionary War made that impossible, and forced Britain to send convicts to another new colonial country, Australia.

The Jews were looking for religious freedom and a better life than they had in Europe. This was in 1733. However, the first Jews who came to Savannah in a sailing vessel were not allowed to come ashore for about two or three months, because they were Jews. They sat in their boat on the Savannah River until the doctor, who was also a passenger, was called to treat those on land. He would not agree to go ashore without the rest of his fellow passengers being granted the same privileges as Oglethorpe's people.

I know my father's family was here in the mid-1800s. I know my mother's family came in that time period, too. There were the other Jews who came to Savannah in the beginning of the 1900s, after the First World War. The Holocaust was a very good reason for Jews to come here. I helped my mother get some of them settled. Some did not get out of their country with much or were not wealthy.

The people who came later were better educated. They had accomplished more prior to their arrival or would never have left

WHO ARE YOU?

Germany, but had no choice. None of them ever went back to Europe to live.

The people who came earlier were just simple people, coming to live free, as well as make their living. Some of them did menial tasks. Many Jews worked in the garment industry in New York, because their families were tailors in Europe. Some were bakers. Then there were the people who sold things from push carts, collecting metal trash to sell, later dealing in steel. Our family came south because there were opportunities here, and we have all fared well.

The Next Sixty-six Years

June 17, 1945, was our wedding day. After the wedding, we went to Santa Barbara to a beautiful hotel. I don't know why, but I signed the register, too. As I leaned over to do so, rice fell out of the brim of my going-away hat. It was the style to wear one in those days. It's funny now, but it wasn't then.

Uncle Reuben got us a room, which was hard to come by during the war, at a hotel in Santa Barbara. It was very pretty, but had a broken bed that fell in. The man who came to fix it said they had been looking for it and got us another one. "Gee, great, thanks," we told him.

That was the first of many new experiences we would have. Herman said I always took everything that happened well, because I loved adventures. He was right. I wasn't afraid of anything because I was with Herman. What we saw of Santa Barbara was beautiful. The rest I'll leave to your imagination.

When we came home to Savannah, for my first time after the war, we stayed for just a little while, going to Miami to stay two weeks in a hotel on the beach for rest and recuperation given to returning soldiers. Phyllis, Cherie, and some of their nurse friends were there, too, in a hotel nearby. Herman got them all dates. I loaned them some of my dresses which didn't fit too well. We all went out to dinner and had a great time. They told me about the operations they had assisted in. I knew I'd made the right decision not to go to nursing school.

One day when I went from the beach to the basement in the hotel, to catch the elevator going up to our room, I ran into a man with POW on his shirt. He was emptying trash cans in this Miami hotel. When I thought of how Herman was treated in Germany, I

The Next Sixty-Six Years

Cherrie, Phyllis, Helen and Herman

Out to dinner in Miami

was furious that this man was even in the USA. Also, if his captors had known Herman was Jewish, they would have sent him to a concentration camp. A lot of Americans who were Jewish POWs were taken by the Germans, sent to Auschwitz where they died. Here was this German POW working in a hotel at the beach in Florida.

After Miami we went to Big Springs, Texas, where Herman was to have pilot training. Some of my mother's family went West in a covered wagon as pioneers—this wasn't much better. The train had hard wicker seats and no air conditioning.

When we got to Big Springs, it was in the middle of the night. Herman had been there before, for his bombardier training. We got off the train; he left me sitting on the suitcases by a street light (near the station) while he ran two blocks to the only hotel in town to get us a room. All the people who got off the train were headed that way, and he remembered that rooms were scarce. When he got to the hotel, it was empty. He got the only cab in town, then came back to get me with all our luggage. I sat there alone, not the least bit afraid. That was 1945. Nobody would do that today.

The war in Japan ended before we left the hotel. When we heard the war was over, people in the hotel opened all the windows and tore pillows apart, throwing the feathers out on the people in the street.

From Savannah to Hollywood

Since we had to stay there until Herman was discharged, the base housing got us a place in a rooming house. We ate out for lunch and dinner. Steak was about the only thing we ate. After being on starvation rations for ten months in prison camp, Herman loved it. I went from ninety-eight pounds to one hundred-eighteen in a couple of months.

At the rooming house where we stayed, there was just one bathroom. The owner had rented the back porch to a mechanic who took his bath every night, never cleaning out the tub. In addition to washing out this grease-covered tub I had to wash and rinse our clothes by hand. Then I had to hang them on a line in the back yard. By the time I got to the last item on the line, the first ones were dry.

Sometimes we could get the taxi to take us to the laundromat to use the washing machine. We had to put our things in the tub, fill up with cold water, wash and then put them through a wringer, turned by hand, after they were washed; you needed to fill up the tub again to rinse the clothes, put them through the wringer again. Herman always helped me. The best help was to cut up my steak at meals, because my wrist hurt from wringing out clothes in the bathtub or turning the washing machine wringer. I mention this because it was a lot different than washing clothes today, but not that different from what Mattie did on Gwinnett Street.

We usually stayed in the movie houses or the Officer's Club, because they were the only places air conditioned. Herman tried to teach me how to play chess. The only thing I remember about that experience was he kept winning. I finally threw the chessmen at him, making that the end of my lessons. He just laughed, deciding it was hopeless. Since the war had ended, Herman was going to be discharged. It was time to go home.

Returning to Savannah, we stayed with my in-laws for a while, and then we moved into an apartment on 42nd Street. We bought a lot in Gordonston, a development on the east side of town. Herman built us a garage apartment on the back of the lot, because we thought eventually we would build a house in the front.

There I was three thousand miles from my home. I had never lived away from my family before. Herman's parents got a divorce.

The Next Sixty-Six Years

I had no relatives in Savannah. I worked at Cranman Insurance Company, answering the phone (I did handle the switchboard in Hollywood) and other important jobs like stamping the mail, but don't ask me about the insurance business. My only comments were and are: "It's not covered, why not?"

Before we settled down to having children, we went to Hartford for two weeks so Herman could study insurance. We stayed in a place owned by one of the large insurance companies. During the day I stayed with the wife of one of the executives. They had a little girl and I would entertain her. We went out with her parents for dinner in the evening. One night we went to eat seafood and I ordered Cherrystone clams, oysters, and ice cream for dessert. The next day Herman went to study at the company, leaving me asleep. When I woke up, my stomach was churning. I started throwing up just as I got to the bathroom. After it was all over, I lay on the bathroom floor and prayed to die. Otherwise it was a really nice trip.

Shortly after that, we went to Atlanta for Herman to continue his studies. I was lucky enough to get a job at Rich's department store. Uncle Reuben came to our rescue again, getting us a room with his sister who lived in Atlanta. I worked in stock control at Rich's; although I had never done anything like that before, it wasn't hard. I rode the streetcar to work. It was winter; the snow was awful. I was glad to come back to Savannah to the warmer weather.

We moved into our garage apartment after it was finished. At that time my Grandpa (Schmalheiser) decided he wanted to go to California to see the family. So I was volunteered to take him. We would fly, which would be his first time in an airplane. We got on the plane; he turned over and went to sleep. He wasn't the least bit afraid. When we were in California, my mother couldn't get me to go anywhere or do anything. When I got back to Savannah, I found out I was pregnant with our first baby, Paul.

I don't know if it was my hormones kicking in, but I got the urge to draw and paint, which I never did before. I got a small book of watercolor paper, a box of eight watercolors and a brush.

From Savannah to Hollywood

While I waited for Paul to be born, I painted the pictures of figurines I had in the apartment. I loved painting, but I had to put that aside for a while, so I could take care of my little one. I learned to play Mah Jong. After Paul was born, I used to take him with me to my games. We all brought our babies. He was still so little, he just slept or had a bottle.

My life in Savannah was quite different from that in Beverly Hills—the Sunset Strip, working in the agency, going to lunch at Schwab's drugstore. Savannah was not glamorous. We were very happy. The only thing I really missed was my family and the beauty of California.

We never did build a house on the front of our lot, because we wanted to move to a part of town where more of our friends lived. We sold our garage apartment in 1948, and bought a house which was in the process of being built on East 59th Street. It had a living room, dining room, kitchen, three bedrooms, one bath, a front porch and a garage. Wow, it was really wonderful.

Lots of people from the community lived there and Herman's father lived a block away. He came to see Paul (who was born July 17, 1947) every day on his way to work, always bringing some toy for him.

Herman and Helen with Lynn, Paul, and Roy

Then Lynn Patricia Cranman was born, May 23, 1950. She had the same big dark eyes, only they were larger and beautiful. She had her daddy's dimples. Her smile was just wonderful and I enjoyed her because the Cranman's always had boys, so I figured she would be my only girl, which she was. She had lovely blonde curls, too.

While we were there, Herman stayed in the Air Force Reserve. He had to fly once a month to be on flying status. Our house was about a mile from the Hunter Field gate. One day when Herman went on a flight, I heard sirens of all kinds going that way. A thought crossed my mind, "Was that at Hunter?" But I went on doing whatever I was involved in.

Later on that day, Herman came home saying he wasn't near a window in the plane, but they had a technical difficulty, not being able to get their wheels down; fortunately, after a while they did. When he got off the plane, he was greeted by a fire truck, an ambulance, and other equipment. He decided to get off flying status, saying he had already used up one of his lives, and he didn't know how many more he had. Then he was called back to active duty to serve in the Korean War.

We lived on 59th Street for two years. Herman was the Base personnel affairs officer. At one point he went to Topeka, Kansas, and I decided to go to California while he was gone. I made our reservations, packed our clothes, got food for the children and bottles for Lynn. We managed all the way to Atlanta. Lynn was eighteen months old, Paul was four-and-a-half. As long as Paul had Whitey, his stuffed toy, he was happy. If Lynn was eating or taking a bottle, she behaved.

When I got on the plane to L.A. that day, it was filled with a group of people making all kinds of noise and ordering drinks. One of the ladies in the group came up to me and said she would hold Lynn if I needed some help, which she did. My double seat was the last one in the back of the plane. Behind us was a half circle of seats where people could come to smoke. I put Lynn to sleep on my two seats, putting Paul on one of the double seats in the smoking section. I curled up on another. I covered them with the blankets we were given and put the pillows under their heads. I put my coat under my head, and we all went to sleep.

In a little while I felt someone put a blanket over me. This gentleman sat down in the only place left, lighting a cigarette. I sat up; we started to talk. He asked me why I was going to California. I told him to see my parents. He asked me what my husband did. I told him insurance. He said his family was in the same business, which was what he was supposed to do. Instead, he and a friend went to Los Angeles, getting jobs in one of the aircraft factories. Every day at lunch and every night they wrote comic scripts. He was in Atlanta with a group of comedians and singers to do a show. He told me the woman who held Lynn for me was Helen O'Connell, the singer. I loved her music, especially "Green Eyes."

The plane trip ended. I told him my name and he told me his. He was Norman Lear, who became one of the most important television producers in Hollywood. We didn't have television then, but I later on found out who he was. I had met lots of people in the industry, so I don't know why that was such a special moment for me, meeting him, but it was. He was so kind, looking out for the children and me.

We started to build our house on Brandywine Road in 1952, which was the beginning of all our unusual houses. We had a cathedral ceiling in the living-dining room. We built three bedrooms, two baths, a den, later adding a studio for me. We lived there for twenty-one years. There were fifty-eight children living on that block, so even though we had friends and children on Columbus Drive, the new house and neighborhood was even better. I continued with all my activities and those of the children.

One time Lynn played the lead in a Christmas play called *The Crocheted Cat*. She was very good, having a sweet little voice. I made her costume out of a pink cotton blanket that looked like it was crocheted. She danced well. When she went to the University of Georgia, she was in the college ballet, also being voted Miss Legs of UGA, but she decided to become a speech pathologist, graduating with honors.

She met and married David Reeves from West Point, Georgia. They came to Savannah after living in South Carolina for a while. David's degree was in landscape architecture, which he practiced for a time and then he went into other businesses. They have three children, Kasey, Joshua, and Morgan.

The Next Sixty-Six Years

Paul went to Benedictine, the local military school administered by the local priests. His uncles, his great uncle, and all his father's first cousins went there, also. It was not his cup of tea and he graduated from the local high school. He went to Georgia State, but came home after a semester. Eventually he went to volunteer for the Air Force. The woman at the draft board said, "Are you Helen's son?" When he said yes, she told him to come home to ask me if it was all right for him to sign up. He came home, walking down the hall kicking the walls. He stormed into my bedroom saying, "Do you have to know everyone in town? The lady at the draft board knew you. She sent me home to ask you if I could volunteer. Unbelievable."

"Go back. Tell her I said 'yes'."

So he did. He was asked if he wanted to go to pilot training, officers' training school, and some other places. He said he wanted to do his two years and get out. This was during the Vietnam War. His years at Benedictine helped him, because the Air Force made him a military policeman. After serving his time, he came home, went to the University of Georgia, graduated with honors, and married his wife, Karyn Shusterman. He went to work at Cranman Insurance agency. They had three children, Matthew, Erin, and Jordan. They lost Matthew, the oldest, to cancer when he was twenty-four. He was a wonderful young man. None of us will ever be the same.

Roy Maurice Cranman was born November 1, 1955, when Paul was eight and Lynn was five. I wanted another baby, thinking also it would be helpful for them to have another sibling because they were getting to be like two only children. It

Roy, Lynn, and Paul

turned out quite different. Roy became the only child. He was good as gold, though.

He did well in school as they all did. He became outstanding at golf, where he still excels. He married Debbie Toland. They had three children and after eighteen years they were divorced. Roy's children stayed with him until they were grown and out on their own—they are Coby, Micah, and Adria.

My favorite story about Roy is when he was about nine. He came to me asking if he could have the piece of black fake fur, left over from a costume I had been making for a play at the Little Theater. I gave it to him, not asking why he wanted it. He sewed the edges down and later on brought it to me, because he wanted me to have a fur stole. That was his personality. It still is.

Roy was born after we had moved to the house we built on Brandywine Road. We lived there for twenty-one years, when we built a house in the county. We stayed there for six years.

The Landings on Skidaway Island became available in the seventies. So we bought a lot over there, built another house that was very open with a swimming pool indoors, which you could see from most of the rooms in the house, and lived there for thirty years. It went so fast. Our last residence is now at Buckingham South, an assisted living facility

One thing I have neglected to mention is the places we went in our travels. I can't remember them all, but they included France, Italy, Israel, Hong Kong. Hawaii, Mexico, Alaska, all over the Caribbean, all over the United States; everywhere between Boston, New York, and Miami on the East Coast, everywhere between Seattle and Cancun on the West Coast. We took oiur children with us to many places, and later our grandchildren. It was a lifetime of fun.

What I Did For the Community

At one of our recent family gatherings, the grandchildren were looking at a book put out by our local Jewish Educational Alliance (JEA, the Jewish Community Center). One of my granddaughters asked me why I wasn't in the book. I told her we just didn't give any information or pictures to the lady who was putting the book together. It's true I haven't done anything lately, but I did work all my life doing things for Savannah's Jewish population and the city, too.

The Jewish Educational Alliance was started in 1912 as a vehicle to help immigrant families that came to Savannah assimilate into American life. It ended up being a facility for the entire community. Today it's open to anyone who would like to participate.

My first experience with the old JEA was when it was located on Barnard and Charlton Streets, a location within walking distance of everyone in the Jewish community. Mother used to take me with her to help make food for the different events held there. I can remember peeling the potatoes for the Mother-Daughter Banquet. I was so little I had to sit on the table to be able to put the potatoes into the big bowl. It was always a mystery to me how Momma let me hold a paring knife at that age.

When my mother became president of the JEA Women's Club, then I was really pressed into service. In addition to peeling potatoes, we did table decorations. Just little things, but we always volunteered for something.

My life revolved around that building with kindergarten, gym classes, drama classes, Sunday School (for a while), and girls' clubs. In later years I went to dances sponsored by the USO, held there for the Jewish soldiers stationed in Savannah during WWII. A volunteering job I enjoyed!

After I was married in 1945, and moved back to Savannah from California, I once again became associated with the JEA. I worked on committees giving input on the new building at 5111 Abercorn Street. I became a Girl Scout and Boy Scout leader, volunteering there for other things, too. Our children also went to kindergarten there, as did the grandchildren and now our great-grandchildren, as well.

Helen at Little Theater production

When our children grew up, I had already become interested in other things. I loved art, working with the Savannah Art Association. I volunteered in the local Little Theater, taking our children there, where we all played parts. I was not like my mother, who was always president of something; she had a real business head. Our sons and daughter are like her and their own father, in that they are business-oriented, too. Our daughter became the second woman president in the history of the JEA organization. In 2011 she was the president of her synagogue, Agudith Archim.

In 1971 we moved into the county, which took us away from the Jewish community. We lived on the Moon River. Johnny Mercer had a house there and wrote his song about it. He was a friend of mine and we corresponded until he died.

I realized many years ago that it was time for the younger people to take over the job of community work. Today we go to lots of fabulous programs held at the JEA. Herman has served on all kinds of committees for things in town. I've volunteered for committees for the city, Mickve Israel Synagogue, Alzheimer Association, Boy Scouts, Girl Scouts, Hadassah, B'nai Brith, Little Theater, United Way, Savannah Art Association, Landings Art Association (I am one of the founders), the Cancer Society, and others.

My First Trip to Washington, D.C.

I was excited to be going to meet Herman in Washington. He had been gone two whole weeks. He was in Hartford learning about insurance, so we decided to meet in Washington. I got off the plane, going to the airlines main desk to check my reservations back to Savannah. After that I took a cab to the hotel to wait for him.

We had a whole weekend together. He said his course was going well. We hadn't been married very long. We were set to have a glorious couple of days. It was cold but didn't rain. We went everywhere.

When we were in the Capitol building, a man came up, saying he would show us around the building, which he did. Then he took us to lunch in the Senate Dining Room. We offered to pay him, but he refused. He said he just enjoyed being able to take visiting people around on the weekends.

When the weekend was over, Herman took me to the airport, saying, "I won't come in with you, because I have to drive all the way back to Hartford. Is that all right?"

"Of course, I'll be fine."

I got out of the car, waved at him and walked bravely into the airport terminal. I don't know why, but for some reason I was very afraid and rightly so. I went up to the airline check-in desk, got in line. When it was my turn I stepped up to the desk, put my ticket on the counter. The clerk looked at my ticket, saying something I didn't understand. He put up his thumb, waving to his left.

"I beg your pardon," I said.

He said it again waving his thumb to the left. The man behind me tapped me on the shoulder, pointing to a neon sign, which said, STAND BY. The desk clerk looked at me like I was an idiot.

"Lady, that means you have to go to the stand-by desk because you don't have a seat on this airplane. If the plane is not filled up, then they will put you on the plane."

There I was in Washington, D.C., by myself, where I didn't know a soul. I had never been in that position in my life. I had five dollars in my pocket; couldn't call my husband. I made up my mind. I definitely wasn't going to the stand-by desk. I looked at the man, saying, "It was you I checked with on Saturday to make sure I had a seat. You confirmed my reservation."

"Listen, lady, I see thousands of people every day, I don't remember you."

"Well, I remember you." Then I had a brilliant moment.

"If you don't give me my seat, I'm gonna scream as loud as I can." I took a deep breath, drew myself up, getting ready.

"Wait a minute." he said, "I just found your reservation." He handed me my ticket. I ran to get on the plane. When I got to my seat, I started to cry. At that moment a man took the seat next to me.

"Can I help you?" he asked.

"No, thank you so much for asking." Then I told him my story. He told me some people who don't have a seat will give the clerk a ten- or twenty-dollar bill, then the clerk will give them someone else's seat and put that person on stand-by. "You did the right thing."

I acted correctly at that moment. Desperation can sometimes make you respond in the right manner. In my entire life I had never been on my own like that. I pretend to Herman to be so brave.

Nancy Hanks, the Train

The name of the train that went from Savannah to Atlanta was the *Nancy Hanks*. It was not named for Abe Lincoln's mother. Not in the Deep South. It was named for a race horse which was named for Lincoln's mother. A huge portrait of our Nancy Hanks, the horse, hung proudly in the dining car of the train.

My memory of the train, which ran from Savannah to Atlanta in the fifties and sixties, was brought to mind when I saw an article in the newspaper. It's been many years since the train ran, but when it did, it was an exciting event for us young mothers to go to Atlanta for the day.

We would get up very early on the day we were going. The train left for Atlanta at 6:00 a.m. Someone's husband took us to the train. It would be cold but it felt good.

About 9:00 a.m. we'd head for the dining car. The waiter was an old friend. We sat at the tables with white tablecloths, white cloth napkins, coffee and tea served in shiny little silver pots. We talked, ate, looked out of the windows at the countryside, and ordered a big breakfast: melon first, next waffles, butter, syrup, and a side of bacon. We ate leisurely, gossiped, put on makeup. We arrived in Atlanta, ready for action at the stores.

When we got off the train, we'd put our coats in a locker, then crossed the street to Rich's department store. We'd start in the basement. That was a good place to pick up socks, underclothes for the children, whatever fit into our budget. Then we went on up to each floor. The furniture floor was my favorite. My more affluent friends went to look at the diamonds and fur coats. We'd work our way to the top floor Tea Room for lunch, where we'd have chicken salad with apples and pecans, sliced date nut bread with cream cheese on it. Then maybe we would have sherbet for dessert.

If we'd bought too much to carry around, we'd run across the street to the train station to stash our stuff in the lockers. When it got close to 6:00 p.m., we got our purchases and get on the train. The ride back was always fun. You'd meet people you knew or made friends with those you didn't know.

As soon as we put our things away, we'd go to the club car, where we would have a glass of wine. Afterward we went to the dining car. The same waiter helped us choose dinner. We took our time ordering, eating, or having another glass of wine. Then we went back to the club car where we talked, telling jokes until the train was home again at midnight. One of the husbands would pick us up.

The story doesn't end there. You see, on the way to Atlanta and upon returning, about halfway between Savannah and Atlanta, the conductor always came through the cars, calling, "Wadley, Wadley, anyone for Wadley?" Then the train would slow down but never really stopped. We always got the giggles, because Wadley had an electric wire with a bulb hanging from it in the middle of a street. It wasn't even a street light.

The train station at Wadley

One year a friend of mine picked me up in Savannah. She took me to her home in Swainsboro, a couple of hours from Savannah. She told me I could go back home on the *Nancy Hanks*. That sounded good to me. After I visited for two days, baked two cakes for my husband, and got some things from her store, I was ready to leave for home. I knew it would be late in the evening when I would be getting on the train. My friend, her husband, and I got in the car to go to the train station, or so I thought.

Nancy Hanks, the Train

"Well," my friend said, "you know we have to ride over to Wadley, the train doesn't come through here."

"You mean the train will stop for me in Wadley? I've never seen it stop. It just slows down."

"It'll stop," they both said.

So we went to Wadley. There wasn't anyone anywhere. We parked by the railroad tracks next to a little building that said "Wadley." The same light was hanging from the power line in the middle of the street. We sat in the car trying to make conversation, but I was so scared. It was like being on another planet.

There was a rumble. My friend said "The train's coming."

We got out hurriedly. I stood by the tracks with my suitcase, the box with my purchases and the two cakes. The train came, slowing down. From Car 2, the conductor got off, bringing a metal step which he put on the ground for me to step on when the train stopped. I mean when it slowed down.

The conductor threw my suitcase and my box with the two cakes on the train. As I stepped on the metal step, the conductor and my friend's husband lifted me onto the train. I leaned my head out of the train, saying my goodbyes. Of course, after that I knew how people got the train at Wadley. Believe me when I tell you it never stopped.

When I got home, I got off the train, so thrilled with the two cakes for my Honey. He looked at me with this hurt look saying, "So what did the two of you do? Talk ugly about me?"

"Well," I thought, "he'll be sorry when he sees the cakes." He was.

When Herman Gave Me Chocolate Candy

To say that you have been married to the same man for seventy years usually astounds people. To have known him for eighty-plus years is even more of a shocker in this day of divorce or live-in partners. To get along is even more of a miracle.

One night at a party, when asked how long Honey and I had known each other, I told my usual story:

Well, let me see, eighty-three years. Yes, that's right. I was five and he was six. He moved across the street from me. Up until that time I had been playing dolls, hopscotch, jump rope, or some other female pursuit. When he came on the scene, I left my girl friends, heading over to sit on his doorstep; just waiting for him to come out to play. He wouldn't even look at me, because he didn't really know any girls, but his mother told him to be polite, which he was.

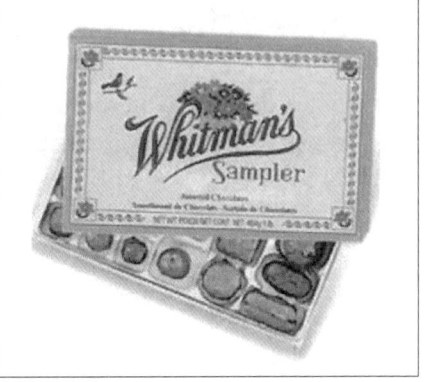

One day I was sitting on his front stoop. He lived on the first floor of this apartment house, which had a porch on the front. This particular day he came out on the porch with a box of Whitman's chocolates. He was startled to see me sitting there. He said, "Would you like a piece of chocolate?" I remember thinking, that if I said yes, he'd have to come out on the stoop to bring it to me. "Yes, I'd like a piece." I answered. I really didn't want any, but chocolate was about the only thing I really liked to eat.

When Herman Gave Me Chocolate Candy

He went inside the house while I waited, humming a little tune, "He's coming. He's coming. Yes, he is." I heard feet coming down the front hall. It was summer, the door was open. I looked up excited with anticipation. Horrors, it wasn't him at all; it was his four-year-old brother, Alvin, who was the bearer of the candy box. I took my piece of candy and went home, throwing it in the gutter as I went.

Sixty years after the incident I told the chocolate candy story, and people laughed as they always do.

We went home, got undressed, got in bed, kissing each other good night. I turned off the light to go to sleep. Honey was asleep in a couple of minutes, while I twisted and turned, unable to go to sleep. Finally, I sat up, turning on the light. He jumped up, saying, "Wuz the matter? Huh, wuz the matter?"

"Why did you send Alvin with the candy instead of coming yourself? Why did you send Alvin with the candy?" I asked again, in a very annoyed tone.

"Why did I send Alvin with the candy? Why did I send Alvin with the candy? What are you beefing about; you got your candy, didn't you?" And he turned over, going right back to sleep.

The Rest of the Story

My Honey

The only time in our lives we were separated was when Herman was in the Army and a POW. He was still always there in my mind and heart. Where we grew up in the Deep South, I went out with many fellows. I was fortunate, because in my family there were never any old maids.

My sisters, my cousins, and I had our pick of the young men to  date. Savannah had two Army bases during WWII. There were lots of young men around. It was our patriotic duty to entertain them, right? So I had fun, but I knew Herman would always love me; also, he would let me love him.

I've always been proud of him, no matter where we went, because in addition to his good looks, he dresses immaculately and smells good naturally. We share the same kind of sense of humor, which is very important; accepting the problems one has to face is a great necessity, too. He is the only fellow I ever dated who went to Benedictine Military School. He looked so sharp, especially in his dress uniform, when he marched in the Saint Patrick's Day Parade.

I remember the day when I decided I would marry him. It was one Sunday afternoon when we had been to the movies. We were teenagers. He had on a white shirt with a striped tie. Afterward we went to Leopold's to get ice cream. We got out of the car and as we crossed the street, I thought to myself, "I'm gonna marry him."

I had on a cotton dress with a big flower on the skirt. After I got married, my mother made an apron out of that dress, giving it to me. I still have it. Not too long ago, I told Herman that was when I decided to marry him. His comment was, "You're just telling me now, after sixty-plus years." Well, I was shy. (It's seventy years, now.)

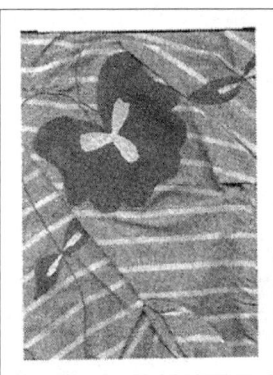

Apron with the big flower

In our day, kissing and hugging was all we did. He never told me he loved me until we got married. I didn't tell him either, because I wasn't sure he loved me. Men didn't express themselves in that manner back in the 1940s. At least not the ones I dated. I certainly couldn't have expressed myself to him.

In the musical *Fiddler on the Roof*, there is a song called "Do You Love Me?" The wife keeps asking the husband if he loves her. Those three little words are sometimes the hardest words to say even when you love someone. Once you do, you want to say it every day in every way.

He's still the same. I'll take him with his minor imperfections any day over all the other nice men I've met in my life. I also knew he would make the best father and husband. He has. It did take a lifetime for both of us to mature. We had many difficulties to overcome, but when you have been married seventy years, it can't be

My Honey

all rosy. We didn't have just a little rain to fall on our parade, we had some real storms. Not between us, just external circumstances.

On that day long ago in Beverly Hills, when I came home from work, my mother told me Herman was missing. I had a terrible feeling in the pit of my stomach. "What have I done?" I let him go never telling him what he meant to me. We were just so young. Can you imagine him coming back, being told I was married to someone else? I still get sick today just thinking about it. Later when we heard he was a prisoner of war, the fear of his being hurt was always with us. My friends who are widows tell me that I don't know what it's like to lose your husband. Well, I lost Herman before I ever had him. Therefore, I appreciate him even more.

Most of the civilians in Europe were very unkind. Herman bailed out of his airplane, which was on fire, in enemy territory (landing without a scratch). The first thing they asked him was if he was Jewish. He was lucky, they just beat him up. Fortunately, he was turned over to the authorities. He says he only did his duty. That's what all WWII people who served say. We count the times he didn't get killed, amazing.

Herman with the news photo of the ship he came home on

He did come home with some emotional scars, but he's too normal and sane to be affected. He wrote his book for the children. Now I'm doing the same. Our family is one of good, kind, decent people. We are a laid-back group, who like it that way. Our children and grandchildren are self-supporting, loving, hard-working, thoughtful, handsome, beautiful, and good natured. I could say much more, but people would just think I was exaggerating.

Our First Grandson, Matthew

He was the oldest son,
Of the oldest son,
Of the oldest son.
He was the first grandchild,
He took his place in the family
    graciously.
He lived it with honor.
Fair of face, beauty of body
Eyes that glowed and
Most always a happy face.
He really was just a normal
    boy,
But beautiful in heart and soul
With some mischief to keep
Things interesting.
Those who met him never
    forgot.
Friends and strangers always
Approached us with a Matthew story to tell.
They are stories of his compassion
And love for others.
Three rabbis spoke with an eloquence
We could not begin to match.
How he changed people's lives
Because of his spiritualism and
Beliefs in Judaism, he made a
Whole community aware.
He brought hope to others.
But I speak with a heart that
Will never mend.
He lived only twenty-four years.

Our First Grandson, Matthew

People say he did what G-d sent him
To do in the time he was given.
That was true, but he would have
Had a wonderful life ahead of him.
He came from long line of good stock,
Good decent people.
He's also being followed by the same,
Other grandchildren who are
Good, kind and honorable.
He was our crown prince.
All the younger grandchildren
Looked up to him
They loved him and he loved them.
We'll all do our best for him
As he did through all his terrible pain
And suffering.
The last thing he said to me
The day before he died was:
"Grandma, it's not fair."
"No," I said, "It's not fair, my darling,
No, it's not fair."

Helen Cranman, grandmother
December, 1997

And the Children, Grandchildren, Great-Grandchildren

Our family now consists of:

Paul and Karyn Shusterman Cranman (our older son)

Karyn and Paul Cranman

Matthew Cranman, their son (deceased)

- Erin (their daughter) and her husband, Brandon Witkow
  Matthew and Ethan, their sons, and daughter
  Eliana Lauren (born October 9, 2015)

Jordan Cranman, Paul and Karyn's younger son

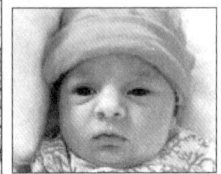

Children, Grandchildren

Lynn (our daughter) **and David Reeves,** her husband

- David (top center) and Lynn (in front of David)
- Joshua Reeves (their son), wife Amanda and their triplets – Evan, Ray, Charles (top row with David)
- Kasey (their daughter) and husband Daniel Berman (right side)
  - Laney and Will, (their children, in front of them)
- Morgan (their daughter) and her husband, Scott McGhie (left side)
- Jackson (their son, next to Will, front) and Ella (in Morgan's lap)
  - Harper (their daughter, next to Morgan)

From Savannah to Hollywood

Roy Cranman, our younger son,
and his family

Coby (Roy's older son) and Mali Cranman

Roy Cranman

Moncie, their son

*Adria (Cranman),
Roy's daughter, and
Lior Moshe, her husband*

*Micah Cranman,
Roy's second son*

CHILDREN, GRANDCHILDREN

*With our children and spouses on our 70th wedding anniversary and my 90th birthday
L to R: Paul and Karyn, David and Lynn, Roy
Herman and Helen*

*Same day with some of our grandchildren and their spouses
Front: Herman, Helen, Kasey, Daniel
Rear: Morgan, Amanda, Josh, Jordan, Adria, Coby*

How wonderful is that?

Poems

Poems

My love for you is warm
Like the beach sun on my back
My love for you is cool
Like a rippling little brook
My love for you sparkles
Like a raindrop on a leaf
And my love for you is gargantuan
In proportions beyond belief
My love for you is a fire
Whose embers will never grow cold
For, Darling, I am your Mother
And you are seven years old

1962

Hair that's golden
Cheeks with pink
A smile that dazzles
Big eyes with a wink

She dances like an elf
She looks like a flower
She thinks like an angel
Her beauty grows by the hour

She has love to offer
As much as is in this world
Take it, you won't be sorry
I know because she's my girl

From Savannah to Hollywood

When you were born
And they brought you to me
I held you close
But you struggled to be free
And my own body trembled
Like an autumn leaf on a tree

Then time passed quickly
You had just turned three
You bruised yourself
It was your knee
I kissed the hurt
Then set you free

Next came the day you were six
Lunchbox fillings I had to fix
Then opened the door
On a world, suddenly so big to me
You went, I smiled
And waved for all to see

At nine came Cub Scouts
An overnight hike
Twelve brought the Soap Box Derby
You won, but, oh, how I wished
You'd stuck with your bike

Now, my son, that you're sixteen
I cannot believe you really belong to me
You're six feet tall, I'm
five foot three

Darling, bend down
And kiss your Mommy!!

1963

Poems

One moment
　of peace
Is all I ask
One
　moment
　　of quiet
from my task
　But
days will come
And
days will go
and little things
　Into big monuments grow.
Time is short
　　　At least for me
I'll not live to "93"
　but
since Motherhood
　is what I chose
My G-d, there's only one thing
　I ask of Thee:
Please,
Let my children outlive me.

I'll love you today
　I'll love you tomorrow
And
　In a thousand years
　But all I'll have
In return for my love
Is
　Tears
　　　Tears
　　　　　Tears

From Savannah to Hollywood

My Friend,
If your Id and Ego were equally as big
You'd only get half as far.
And all along the way
YOU and YOURSELF would argue
About how great YOU REALLY ARE!!!!

All the while
the female crows strutted
back and forth
in front of the little sparrow

Proud they were
and knowing their beauty
thinking
the peacock
was dying for their
love

But the little sparrow
knew what they did not
that
the peacock
only loves the
peahen

If you wuz a dog
Then I'd wish I wuz a flea
Cawse no matter where you went
Then that's jus' where I wud be
And you cud scratch and scratch
But you'd never get rid of me
If you wuz a dog an' I was a flea

Poems

MY LOVE
is all I have
of my very own
to give
IT CANNOT BE TAKEN FROM ME
Life to me is just a dream
and I
Well, I, its' greatest dreamer
YOU
you are the tear drops on my cheek
I BEG OF YOU
do not forsake me
For I will give my
love to you FOREVER
Because
there is no way for me to say "No"
And with my "Yesses"
I am swept away in
a tide of anonymity
to a windswept rock
Where
only sometimes
the sun shines
to warm
the crown of my soul

It must be marvelous . ... to think you're great!!
It must be marvelous   to think you rate!!
And the way to make this really true
Is to look in your mirror and say:
"You are, you will be". . . and you do
THINK YOU'RE GREAT!!!!!!

From Savannah to Hollywood

The sun, the sky,
the sand, and the sea

A painting in time.
G-d's gift to me.

The waves sounding
on the shore.

Birds winging.
Breezes singing.

This to love,
So much to adore.

The sea shells vivid
with nature's beauty.

The beach washed to look
like an abstract tree.

All part of HIS unfinished symphony.

Some people speak
Spanish
Some people are
 veddy British
But the person
 who fractures me the most
Is my friend
 who speaks Rebel Yiddish!

Poems

Did you ever feel
suspended in
time and space?

Thinking you could
see G-d
face to face?

Just for a moment...
Wanting to ask a question or two
"Tell me, G-d, your purpose for me?"
"Tell me, G-d, what to do?"
Then as you reach out
to touch
His face
He disappears
and you're
left …………..

Suspended
  in
   time
  and
   space

From Savannah to Hollywood

Today
is tomorrow
Tomorrow
is forever
And in my palm I hold
All my today and tomorrows
    That are
          never
                never
                      never

As I looked my adversary
in the face
I wished I could be airborne
somewhere in space
And as I received each verbal blow
I felt the animosity inside me grow
Waiting to answer
this evil peer
While pushing back
each and every tear
And then   a fuse within me blew
I smiled
kept quiet

But my heart cried out:
"TO HELL WITH YOU!"

Poems

Paul sez . ...
Momma, I can't date Jody
for sho'
Cause she's fo' fut six
An' I'm six fut fo'

A wheel is round
A block is square
But what shape is fear?
Or even despair
The sky is blue
The grass is green
But, what color does happiness seem?
A yard is long
An inch is short.
How long are lies? Can truth be bought?
Only age can bring worries
Of love
   despair
         happiness
               lies or
                    truth
And, oh,
how I long
   for
my prismatic
   cylindrical
youth

My Paintings

My Paintings

Helen at an exhibit of her work

Forsyth Park Fountain

The Wedding Song

FROM SAVANNAH TO HOLLYWOOD

Ma Belle Amie

Death of JFK

The Concert

My Paintings

Last Day of Summer

A Tree All Alone

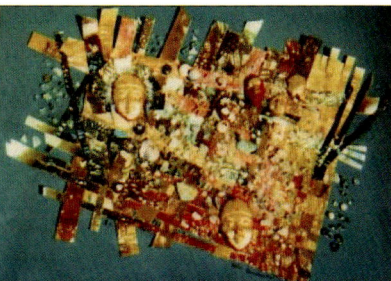

Abstract Weave

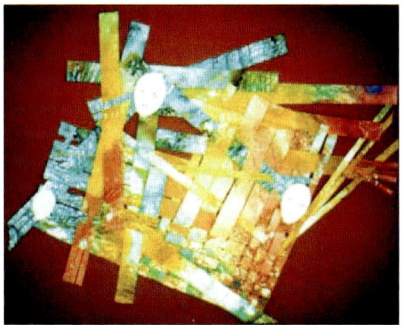

Crisscross

From Savannah to Hollywood

Moses Leading the Jews Our of Egypt

The Rabbis

River Street

My Paintings

Alien Hero

Undersea Scene

King Solomon and Queen Esther

From Savannah to Hollywood

Flower Sale

Summer Colors

Savannah Chair

My Paintings

Madame Butterfly

Indian Dream

Isle of Hope Church

From Savannah to Hollywood

Water, Sand, and Sea

Firewood and Flowers

My Paintings

Look, He's Caught a Fish

Helen's painting for the cover of Herman's book,
A Measure of Life